# ROBERT R. CHURCH JR. AND
# THE AFRICAN AMERICAN POLITICAL STRUGGLE

UNIVERSITY PRESS OF FLORIDA

Florida A&M University, Tallahassee
Florida Atlantic University, Boca Raton
Florida Gulf Coast University, Ft. Myers
Florida International University, Miami
Florida State University, Tallahassee
New College of Florida, Sarasota
University of Central Florida, Orlando
University of Florida, Gainesville
University of North Florida, Jacksonville
University of South Florida, Tampa
University of West Florida, Pensacola

# Robert R. Church Jr. and the African American Political Struggle

DARIUS J. YOUNG

University Press of Florida

Gainesville · Tallahassee · Tampa · Boca Raton
Pensacola · Orlando · Miami · Jacksonville · Ft. Myers · Sarasota

Publication of this work made possible by a Sustaining the Humanities through the American Rescue Plan grant from the National Endowment for the Humanities.

First cloth printing, 2019
First paperback printing, 2022

27  26  25  24  23  22    6  5  4  3  2  1

Library of Congress Cataloging-in-Publication Data
Names: Young, Darius J., author.
Title: Robert R. Church Jr. and the African American political struggle / Darius J. Young.
Description: Gainesville : University Press of Florida, 2019. | Includes bibliographical references and index.
Identifiers: LCCN 2018029685 | ISBN 9780813056272 (cloth) | ISBN 9780813069449 (pbk.)
Subjects: LCSH: Church, Robert Reed, Jr. 1885–1952. | Memphis (Tenn.)—Politics and government—History. | African American politicians—Tennessee—Memphis. | African American labor leaders—Tennessee—Memphis.
Classification: LCC F444.M59 Y68 2019 | DDC 324.2092 [B] —dc23
LC record available at https:// lccn.loc.gov_2018029685

The University Press of Florida is the scholarly publishing agency for the State University System of Florida, comprising Florida A&M University, Florida Atlantic University, Florida Gulf Coast University, Florida International University, Florida State University, New College of Florida, University of Central Florida, University of Florida, University of North Florida, University of South Florida, and University of West Florida.

University Press of Florida
2046 NE Waldo Road
Suite 2100
Gainesville, FL 32609
http://upress.ufl.edu

This book is dedicated to my grandparents Mary Long, James Senior, and Bertha Young.

# CONTENTS

# FIGURES

# ACKNOWLEDGMENTS

For the past decade I have researched the life and career of Robert Reed Church Jr., and along this journey many people have contributed their talents, time, and resources. I would like to begin by thanking Dr. Aram Goudsouzian, who encouraged me to consider Church as a possible re-search topic. I had just moved to Memphis a few months earlier and knew little about the city's history. After some convincing, I decided to learn more about this fascinating figure, and I have been studying him ever since. I thank "Dr. G." for challenging me as a writer, researcher, and criti-cal thinker. His guidance, advice, and enthusiasm have made me a better scholar and historian.

I am also grateful for the support, suggestions, and criticism of my other professors at the University of Memphis. Beverly Bond echoed the suggestions of Dr. G and encouraged me to research the Church family. Her work on Tennessee women and Roberta Church helped me better under-stand the contributions of the Church women to Robert Church Jr.'s life and career. It was always a pleasure talking Memphis history with Charles Crawford. He is the leading Memphis historian; his knowledge of the city is unparalleled, and my project benefited immensely from his guidance. His personal reminiscing friendship with Roberta Church helped me gain a more intimate understanding of the Churches and their contributions to Memphis.

I would also like to thank Arwin Smallwood for his support and men-torship over the years. To Sarah Potter, your comments challenged me to think more critically about the overall direction of my work and helped me place Church in a broader historical context. I would also like to give special recognition to D'Ann Penner, who provided me with summer fel-lowships with the Benjamin L. Hooks Institute for Social Change, which allowed me to concentrate on my research. Her work as an intellectual, author, activist, and humanitarian is inspiring. I am forever grateful for the funding I received from the Department of History at the University of Memphis.

I also enjoyed the camaraderie of my classmates at the university. We challenged each other inside and outside of the classroom, but still made time for fun and laughs. I especially want to thank Shirletta Kinchen, whose friendship and advice I cherish deeply. Her work on the Black Power movement in Memphis has been impactful and started new conversations about black activism in the Bluff City.

I appreciate the comments and suggestions from the reviewers. Your feedback has made my work stronger. To my editor, Sian Hunter, thank you for being so patient and nurturing this book to completion. I could not have asked for a better publishing experience for my first book. Special recognition also goes out to the entire team at the University Press of Florida.

The great civil rights activist Fannie Lou Hamer often reminded us "never to forget where we came from and always praise the bridges that carried us over." In that spirit, I would be remiss to not thank my professors at my alma mater, Florida A&M University (FAMU), who challenged me as a student, and today have welcomed me back as their colleague. The late Theodore Hemingway sparked my interest in African American history as a freshman. I certainly miss our conversations in his office, and his unique perspective on the issues that plagued the black community. A simple question, "What's wrong with the black people?" was often the start of long, insightful, and complex discussions about the black experience. His wisdom, insight, humor, and knowledge are surely missed and will always remain with me. Titus Brown challenged me, perhaps more than any other professor, to be a better researcher. His knowledge of archives and their holdings is remarkable, and he has played a vital role in my development as a historian. Dr. Brown remains a close adviser and mentor, and I would like to thank him for investing so much of his time and wisdom in my development as a scholar.

Canter Brown pushed me as a writer and helped me publish my first article as a graduate student. Thanks for opening up your home archives to me as a graduate student. Larry Rivers and his sustained publishing record as a professor, dean, and the eighth president of the Ft. Valley State University, helped to establish a high standard in our department, and I am truly lucky to be able to call on him as a colleague and mentor.

Attending FAMU is one of the best decisions I have made, and I am truly grateful for my experiences on "the highest of seven hills," in Tallahassee, Florida. Walking those hills in the unforgiving Florida sun has a way of building a kinship bond amongst FAMUans, and I am truly privileged to have such a strong network of Rattlers in the field. Drs. Reginald Ellis, Shirletta Kinchen, Will Guzman, Ameenah Shakir, Daleah Goodwin, Christina Davis, Krystal Frazier, Tameka Hobbs, Sheena Harris, Christopher Daniels, Ibram Kendi, Kimberly Brown-Pellum, Daria Willis, and so many others, you all have transformed academic conferences to family reunions. Keep striking, Rattlers!

I have been truly fortunate to work with some great archivists and librarians throughout the country. In particular, I owe a special debt of gratitude to the great Ed Frank, curator of the Mississippi Valley Collection at the University of Memphis. I would also like to thank Gerald Chaudron and his staff for assisting me with the photographs for the book. G. Wayne Dowdy and the archivists and librarians at the Benjamin L. Hooks Public Library were always courteous and helpful, and I could not have completed this work without your knowledge and expertise of Memphis history.

Special thanks to the archivists at Harvard University Archives Library, the Chicago Historical Society, Auburn Avenue Research Library on African American Culture and History, the Schomburg Center for Research in Black Culture, the Tennessee State Archives, and the Library of Congress.

A special thanks to Ansley Abraham and the Southern Regional Education Board's Doctoral Scholars Program. Thank you for the funding I received, which allowed me to be freed of my duties as a graduate assistant and focus exclusively on my studies. However, as the motto states, my experience as a SREB doctoral scholar was certainly "more than a check and a handshake." The support I received at the annual Institute on Teaching and Mentoring provided me with invaluable lessons and strategies to excel in graduate school while preparing for the professoriate. I am honored to be the 567th graduate of this program. And I would also like to thank the Gilder Lehrman Institute of American History for their financial support.

To my friend, colleague, and brother Reginald K. Ellis, thanks your feedback and keen analysis of black leadership during the Jim Crow era. Let us continue to challenge each other to be great, and to move onward and upward in our respective careers. To my mentor, friend, and brother David H. Jackson Jr., you recognized talents in me that I did not see myself. There is no other person more responsible for my pursuing a career as a historian. You continue to be a role model for me both inside and outside of the academy. Thank you for all that you have done to further my career. Dr. Jackson epitomizes what it means to be a mentor. Thanks for everything, good brother.

I am truly fortunate to have a strong support system. I would like to extend a special recognition to my lifelong friends James Rush Jr., Hardy Wilson III, Christopher Brunson, Sean Williford, and Christopher Ward. Although I can't get back to Detroit as often as I would like, whenever I'm home it is like I never left.

Finally, I could not have completed this book without the support of my family. My father, James Young, instilled in me the importance of having a strong work ethic, and taking pride in everything that I do. His teachings and life lessons have molded me into the man that I am today. My mother, Karen Long, always preached the importance of obtaining an education and made unimaginable sacrifices to ensure my success. You were my first teacher, and I am forever thankful for you and all that you have done for me. My sister, Dayna, thanks for putting up with me, and it has been a pleasure to watch my little sister grow into the accomplished young woman, mother, and wife that you are today. Special thanks to LaVerne Young for always being so thoughtful and supportive. I could not have completed this project without the support of my in-laws, Bruce and Edwina Gaynor, whose generosity is unrivaled.

To my wife, Tina, thank you for being so patient and understanding during this process. It has been a wonderful journey so far, and I can't wait to see what the future still has in store for us. Lastly, special thanks to my daughter, Ayanna, and my son, Darius Jr., who are my inspiration.

*Peace,*

*Darius J. Young*

# Introduction

## The Gentleman from Memphis

ROBERT REED CHURCH JR. (1885–1952) often spent his evenings reading in his study at the family's residence on 384 Lauderdale Street in Memphis, Tennessee. Church, a successful businessman, enjoyed going to the theater and occasionally betting on the horses at the race-track. His favorite pastime was quail hunting on the family farm, located near the outer edges of the city. The farm was his sanctuary. He could escape the daily pressures of being a black leader during the Jim Crow era and strategize about his next attempt to organize the black vote. The latter consumed his imagination and became his lifelong passion. His efforts placed him in the discussion of the nation's most influential leaders. Most of his achievements, however, remain largely unheralded.

Church stood at the center of nearly every major black political move-ment during the first half of the twentieth century, despite his often being ignored by historians. At the height of his career, he possessed as much power and influence as many of his better-known contemporaries. Specifi-cally, as a black political leader, he had few rivals. Presidents, congress-men, labor organizers, NAACP officials, businessmen, entertainers, and intellectuals all corresponded with Church and sought his advice about uplifting the race. So, *how is it that we know so little, about someone who has accomplished so much?*[1]

In many ways, Church's legacy is perhaps a victim of his leadership style. He rarely sought attention and instead chose to lead from behind the scenes. Church had a pleasant personality but was naturally a quiet man. A white reporter once described his manner: "courteously frank, his actions bespeak a fair candor. His voice is soft, and his English perfect. While very democratic in his manner, it sometimes is not the easiest thing in the world to gain an audience with a man of national prestige."[2] Church was a complex person. A member of the black elite, a politician, an institution builder, and an activist, Church combined these characteristics to forge a career that helped change the American democratic process. In 1953, the *Journal of Negro History* commented that Church "was always alert and a watchman on the wall in behalf of civil and human rights for Negroes." No person before him had more success in ushering black people to the polls. Throughout his career, he never stopped advocating on behalf of African Americans.[3]

For Church, politics presented the best possibility for black people to fully realize the promises of American Democracy. He interpreted the ballot as the highest representation of freedom, and used the Republican Party as a tool for social change. Historians and other scholars have unfairly categorized Church as a blind follower of the Grand Old Party (GOP). He saw politics as a way of challenging the status quo and forcing white Americans to live up to the promises of the Constitution. America's constitutional framework guarantees the fundamental concept of human equality and human rights. "It is within this conceptual milieu, inherited from the American Revolution, that the Negro has carried on his struggles for social, political and economic emancipation," wrote Ralph Bunche.[4] Church believed the most deliberate approach to obtaining these rights was by challenging the very people who had the authority to interpret, amend, and enforce the Constitution. His lifelong affiliation with the Republican Party demonstrates his pragmatism. Church recognized that African Americans did not have a true advocate from either faction, but he chose to embrace the romanticized myth of the "Party of Lincoln" to convince whites to live up to the ideals of the party, and to inspire African Americans to remain loyal to the party that freed the slaves. Church recognized that black people needed a stage to voice their concerns, and only then could they make their issues a national problem. For most of his career, the Republican Party seemed to be the natural political home for African Americans, since the Democratic Party was not a feasible option for blacks in the South.

Church's role within the party was always as more of an agitator than a supporter. He fought tirelessly to get white Republicans to recognize the plight of African Americans and to serve as their political advocate.

Church's political organization, the Lincoln League of America, represents more of a protest organization than a collection of black GOP loyalists. He founded the Lincoln League as a response to the false promises of party leaders, but more importantly to confront the lily-white factions of the party. In reaction to the league's founding, the *Cleveland Advocate* wrote, "To Robert Church it appeared the time was propitious for a protest voiced by Negro voters."[5] It continued, "Possessing the fighting blood, inherited, a contempt for habitual ignoring of his people by the party managers, he threw himself into the breach." The Lincoln League would grow to serve as essentially the black Republican National Convention throughout the 1920s. It's meetings and conventions showcased the diversity of black leadership. It provided a platform for relatively obscure black Republicans like Roscoe Conkling Simmons, Perry Howard, Henry Lincoln Johnson, and Ben Davis to elevate as leaders in the GOP.

Church's influence and wealth further enabled him to challenge white policymakers without fear of repercussions. Church's political machine allowed him to negotiate basic concessions for the black community on a local level, while continuously challenging the racial consciousness of white Americans nationally. His relentless pursuit of equality helped bring about gradual change. Early on, he identified the political potential of the African American community, and he turned this innate political energy into a solid voting constituency. By enfranchising thousands of African Americans, Church helped hold their elected officials accountable. Church often warned Republicans of the consequences of ignoring their black constituency. During the FDR years, when blacks' political loyalty started to shift, Church blamed the Republicans' lack of concern, not black voters, for their defection from the party. He once remarked that he never intended for all African Americans to be Republicans, "but the majority of Negroes [to] become politically alive."[6] His activism demonstrated the power of black cohesion, and the importance of developing a united stance against white supremacy. As a reporter once wrote, "be of good cheer brother church, you have this day lighted a candle in america which we hope, by god's grace, may never be put out."[7]

*Robert R. Church Jr. and the African American Political Struggle* serves as a lens into the political activity of African Americans during the first half of the twentieth century. It focuses on the strategies that Church used to organize and empower black people through the vote. Church believed that voting served as the most practical approach for African Americans to obtain full citizenship in this country. He remained active until his death in the 1952; however, this book focuses mainly on his activism during the 1910s and 1920s. Through his activism, Church demonstrated the political power of African Americans on a national level. By enfranchising thousands of black southerners and developing a substantial voting constituency, black voters could have their voices heard. Specifically, this book focuses on the incremental victories achieved by black voters, and argues that the activism of Church and his colleagues served as the catalyst for the modern civil rights movement.

# Growing Up Church

ON SUNDAY, OCTOBER 11, 1936, black Chicagoans spilled onto Giles Avenue and formed a crowd in front of the famed Eighth Regiment Armory, located in the Bronzeville District on Chicago's South Side, better known as "The Black Metropolis." They gathered to catch a glimpse of the recent four-time Olympic gold medalist, Jesse Owens, who had dominated the world games that summer in Berlin. Owens came to the Windy City to give a speech in front of a crowd of nearly ten thousand people who had packed the historic establishment. The sprinter, however, did not come to Chicago to bask in the adoration of the city for his athletic accomplishments. Instead, he had stopped to campaign for the Republican nominee for president, Alfred Landon. The Republican National Committee (RNC) wanted to use the Olympic star, who had recently "made world-wide fame for himself, his race, and his country," to encourage black and white Chicagoans to support the Kansas governor, as well as the Republican ticket. After the spectacle of Owens's arrival, the Olivet Choir whipped the crowd into a frenzy with a few gospel selections and brought them to their feet with a solo titled "Win With Landon" performed by Ethel Hargraves. Several key black figures in the GOP, such as Roscoe Conkling Simmons and Oscar DePriest, spoke about the Republican platform, while later declaring that the day be forever remembered as "Jesse Owens Day." Finally, after all the pomp and circumstance, Owens urged the onlookers to "hold fast to the American way of doing things" and support Landon.[1] At the conclusion of the event, more music ensued, and Owens was quickly ushered to the train station to board a "special car" he shared with the most influential black Republican of his era, Robert Church Jr., to continue his tour of the Midwest.

The *Chicago Defender* published a picture captioned "Three Aces Get Together." The photo showed the presidential candidate sandwiched between the sharply dressed Owens and Church while appearing to be having a conversation. Church had served as the main organizer of the multicity tour that had spanned the East Coast and Midwest. He did not give any lengthy speeches or seek any attention during the tour. Instead, Church remained focused on the campaign and mobilizing the black vote. In many ways, The "Owens tour" is symbolic of Church's approach to leadership during his forty-year career in national politics. As the men traveled from city to city, Church remained in the background, visible but quiet.[2]

Instead of clamoring for recognition, Church preferred to function more as a political power broker who used his influence, wealth, and connections to interject the plight of black Americans into the national political discourse. This approach earned Church the respect of the nation's most prominent leaders, black and white. In many ways, this seemed to be his destiny. His parents had nurtured him and his siblings to be leaders in their community. His privileged upbringing, membership in the black elite, education, and training prepared him for a life of political activism. Church's position as a national leader placed him in the center of nearly every major black political struggle during the first half of the twentieth century. Despite his national prominence and political power, he would always be known by those closest to him as the gentleman from Memphis.[3]

## THE CHURCHES AND SOUTHERN BLACK ELITE FAMILIES

Church, the third child of Robert Sr. and Anna Church, was born into a southern black aristocratic family on October 25, 1885, at the family's palatial mansion on Lauderdale Street. By the turn of the century, Church's father had accumulated a fortune through his real estate holdings, which included dozens of properties, an auditorium, a park, and a bank. His parents afforded him and his three siblings an exceptional lifestyle, especially for an African American family during the height of Jim Crow. Despite his unique upbringing, Church remains connected to the common ancestral experience of most African American families, as he is the son of a former slave.

Church Senior was born in Holly Springs, Mississippi, on June 18, 1839, the son of a white slave owner by the name of Charles Beckwith Church, who owned steamboats that shipped goods down the Mississippi River from Memphis to New Orleans. Church Senior knew little about his mother, Lucy, other than that she was sold to a slave-owning family in Louisiana, where she remained until she died in 1851. His upbringing left him either confused or reluctant to embrace his racial background. "How much of a colored man are you?" asked an interviewer in the aftermath of the infamous 1866 Memphis race riots. "I don't know—very little. . . . My father is a white man; my mother is as white as I am. . . . My father owned my mother," he claimed.[4] The family would eventually embrace the idea that they had no African ancestry, and were in fact the descendants of a Malay princess named Emmeline in an effort to distance themselves from the typical slave experience.

The Churches' romantic remembrance of their slave ancestry is more legend than fact; however, it offers insight into the construction of a collective identity shared by southern black elite families in the late nineteenth century. In the retelling of their family's history, the Churches reluctantly acknowledged their connection to slavery while simultaneously distancing themselves from the typical slave experience. The letters emphasize that Emmeline had no African blood, spoke French, lived in cabins away from other enslaved Africans, and worked as a seamstress. Her owners, moreover, never considered her a slave. Both Emmeline and Lucy held positions of distinction on their family's plantations and ascended to the very top of the social hierarchy for enslaved laborers. They rather imply that an aristocracy existed even within the oppressive confines of slavery.[5]

In many instances, a direct link to the "peculiar institution" served as a justifiable reason to deny a person's membership in the black elite, especially in the North. Although skin color, refinement, education, wealth, family pedigree, social organizations, and family prominence remained important qualifiers in both regions, the issue of slave ancestry separates the two. The northern black elite emphasized the ability to trace their family heritage to the relatively small quasi-free black societies in places such as New England, New York, and Washington, D.C. The social status of privileged blacks in the North depended on the number of generations removed from slavery as much as any other factor. The Churches and other southern black elite families did not have this option. Therefore, they embraced the idea of tying their family heritage to privileged slaves who did not typically work in the fields, but instead worked as house servants, domestics, or skilled slaves.[6]

The Churches' embracement of this rendition of their family history offers an intimate portrayal of the process by which southern black aristocratic families constructed and maintained their status for generations. Much of the scholarly discourse that exists on the black elite focuses on their "exclusivity and dominance of black institutions."[7] It implies that their quests to assume leadership positions were motivated solely by self-serving interests. However, this interpretation needs reevaluation. Certain aspects of the social construction of black elite families deserve criticism, and are problematic. However, scholars must also be cautious in categorizing black elites in such broad terms. Certainly, the Church family took calculated measures not only to solidify their status in society, but also to ensure the development of a class of leaders that could impact the larger African American community. Slavery, emancipation, and the rise of the Jim Crow South determined the strategies used by families like the Churches to nurture future leaders. For instance, Church Senior and Anna wanted to spare their children from the humiliating experiences most African Americans suffered in the South. They knew that their children would have to exude confidence and be willing to confront whites in their adult years. They believed that, by subjecting their children to the harsh realities of Jim Crow, they risked harming their children's ability to resist white supremacy in adulthood. During the early civil rights struggles of the twentieth century, a class of nurtured leaders, including Robert Church Jr., shared a collective consciousness with the entire black community.[8]

In the black elite's initial appeals for social recognition, many of its members gradually realized that, despite their ancestry, education, wealth, and any other accomplishments, their status in mainstream American society would ultimately be determined by their race. This barrier became more apparent after Reconstruction, when former white abolitionists abandoned their quest to improve race relations and white supremacists violently "redeemed" the South. In the remaining decades of the nineteenth century, black elites, especially in the South, devised new strategies that eschewed proving their equality to whites. Instead, they established a foundation for African Americans to succeed despite the direst of circumstances. To be included within the black elite, one needed to be a leader. Upper-class blacks no longer solely appealed to whites for approval. Instead they sought the approval of the black community—a possibility only made by expressing genuine concern for their race. The rejection of the black elite by their white counterparts, the establishment of the Jim Crow South, and the violence of white southern terrorism on black society encouraged African Americans to develop a more substantial, congruent society. Families such as the Churches embodied the characteristics of the new southern black elite as evidenced by their family background, accumulation of wealth, educational training, faith, professions, associations with fraternal orders, marriages, and political leadership. The success of Robert Church Jr. reflected the sacrifice of his parents, especially his father.[9]

During the first two decades after Church Senior moved to Memphis, he had a series of ups and downs. He had established several businesses around town, most famously on Beale Street. He had been shot in the head during the 1866 Memphis riots, gotten married and divorced from Louisa Ayers Church, with whom he had two children, Mary and Thomas. He purchased dozens of vacant properties left by fleeing residents during the 1878–79 yellow fever epidemic and purchased the first thousand-dollar bond to restore the city charter in its aftermath. The latter forever endeared him to the city. By the turn of the twentieth century, Church owned numerous residential properties and saloons, along with Church Park and Auditorium. In 1906, he founded the Solvent Savings Bank and Trust Company and established his legacy as the first black millionaire in the South.[10]

Church's parents married in 1885. His mother, Anna Wright, a musician and teacher, had also come from a prominent family. His father essentially "married up" and gained status by marrying into the "fashionable social circle" of the Wright family. Anna's early life eclipsed the extraordinary upbringing of her husband's. Anna was born free in Memphis in 1856 and attended Lemoyne Normal and Commercial School (now Lemoyne-Owen College), where she was one of two members of the inaugural graduation class. She then studied at the Musical Institute at Antioch College in Yellow Springs, Ohio, and attended the Oberlin Conservatory of Music at prestigious Oberlin College. Together their union not only represented a personal union between the two, but also confirmed their elite social status in the black community. Church's parents likely taught him and his younger sister, Annette, what they considered the "cornerstone of respectability . . . thrift, hard work, self-respect, and righteousness," along with the responsibility they had to their race.[11]

In his 1908 directory, *The Bright Side of Memphis,* Green Polonius Hamilton wrote that, "Great as Mr. Church is considered because of his enormous wealth, he is, in the writer's humble judgment, greater because of the high character of his children." Hamilton continued, "no man could wish a greater monument to his memory than the exemplary character and worthy lives of his devoted children."[12] Family served as the core institution for the black elite to preserve their legacy. Parents expected their children to maintain their family's prestige. Most important, the black elite family nurtured a class of African American leaders that secured equal rights for African Americans during the freedom struggles of the early twentieth century.[13]

Robert Senior and Anna viewed education as an agent for social change. On Church's fourth birthday, his older half-sister and women's rights activist Mary Church Terrell wrote him a detailed letter and sent him two books written in German. "Sister wants you to read these little German poems to her when you have a few more birthdays," challenged Mary. "Someday you must go to school and learn a great deal, so that you can speak lots of languages besides know other things. Sister will talk about that when we see each other."[14] She also sent him a silver German coin with the words "Gruss aus Berlin" (Greetings from Berlin) inscribed on it. Mary instructed Robert to wear it as much as possible so he would not lose it.[15]

Church's parents and older siblings often reminded him about the importance of education. They felt it was essential to develop a sense of self-sufficiency through obtaining a liberal arts education to avoid being controlled by whites. This independence was essential to developing a class of leaders and activists who could voice their opinions on race relations without the threat of losing their jobs. Privileged African Americans thus selectively chose schools that reinforced their collective agenda of racial uplift.[16]

Church initially attended the private kindergarten and elementary school of Julia B. Hooks. The Hookses represented one of Memphis's most respected black families. Julia Britton Hooks was an accomplished musician, teacher, and principal. In fact, she and his mother, Anna, often played piano together and performed in classical music concerts during the 1880s. After Hooks opened the Hooks Cottage School in 1892, it quickly became the school of choice for the city's privileged black families. For middle and high school Church attended private black Episcopal parochial schools in Memphis.[17] Church also attended the predominantly white Calvary Episcopal Church, where Bishop Charles Todd Quintard confirmed him at an early age.[18]

The Episcopal Church boasted the largest membership of black aristocrats across the nation prior to the Civil War and maintained a substantial number after Emancipation. The Episcopal Church functioned not only as a place of worship, but also as a place for affluent African Americans to socialize and network. By 1900, only fifteen thousand African Americans worshipped at Episcopal churches, adding to "an image of exclusiveness." George Freeman Bragg, one of the most respected black Episcopal clergyman, "admitted the church still contained a small contingent of maniacal colored people who used the church to get as far as possible from the ordinary Negro."[19] The Episcopal Church also served as the institution of choice for influential whites. Therefore, many of the professional and political relationships that developed between powerful whites and African American leaders originated during service on Sundays. Once the black leader Booker T. Washington told a joke about an elderly black woman from Mississippi who wandered into an Episcopal church, "took a seat in the rear, and began to moan and clap her hands as the rector began his sermon." From there, "Her demonstration practically broke up the service, and one of the officers of the church went back to stop her. 'What's the matter with you aunty, are you sick?' 'No, sir, I'se happy, I'se got religion. Yes, sir, I'se got religion.' The officer then replied, 'Why don't you know that this isn't the place to get religion?'" Black Episcopalians viewed themselves as an exclusive social class as much as a religious denomination. The Episcopal Church as an institution did little to improve race relations in America; however, children such as Church developed the skill to interact and form alliances with prominent leaders, regardless of race, to advance a specific agenda.[20]

The exclusive network of family, church, and school sheltered Church from the degradation that most African Americans faced in the South. The Churches shielded their children from the personal humiliation of the Jim Crow laws and encouraged them to exude confidence and demand fair treatment from whomever they encountered. As a result, children such as Church developed a sense of entitlement. They challenged figures of authority and viewed themselves as equals to whites. Church also learned that his experience was atypical. As a child, he noticed his father only reserved private Pullman accommodations when they rode the train. Church stated that his father did this "not only for comfort but to avoid segregation." He also observed, "It was possible to stop at hotels in the North and East, and that it was possible for all children to attend the same schools in the North and East, but in the South neither of these was possible."[21] The parents of the black elite skillfully developed a sense of social awareness in their children while protecting them, as much as possible, from the humiliation of white supremacy. By traveling across country, the children witnessed a world quite different from the realities of the South. This profoundly affected their views on race and political activism as young people.

As Church prepared for college, he became increasingly aware of his surroundings and developed a deeper understanding of the issues that plagued the black community. In the fall of 1904 he enrolled at Morgan Park Military Academy in Morgan Park, Illinois. The academy served as a preparatory school for the University of Chicago. The school cost the Churches nearly $800 per year for room, board, and books. Church graduated from Morgan Park in 1905 and then followed in his older siblings Mary and Thomas's footsteps by attending Oberlin College in Ohio. Oberlin established its reputation by becoming the first college in the United States to admit African Americans and women. It played an active role during the abolitionist movement and offered an atmosphere "probably freer of prejudice than virtually any other predominantly white institution in the country."[22] Oberlin became a school of choice for the children of the black elite, as evidenced by the school's legacy of producing influential black professionals and leaders. Church remained at Oberlin for two years before completing his academic training at the Packard School of Business in New York City. In New York, he interned for two years on Wall Street, learning the banking industry. Robert planned to then return to Memphis to run his father's Solvent Savings Bank. His educational experience in the North allowed him to observe firsthand the black experience in places such as Illinois, Ohio, and New York. He also developed long-lasting relationships with up-and-coming black leaders such as James Weldon Johnson, and he became more interested in politics.[23]

In 1907, Church returned home confident and optimistic about his future. He immediately began working as a cashier for his father's bank while managing his real estate holdings. Two years later he was elected president of the bank, and applied the knowledge he gained in New York City to the institution his father founded. Church seemed poised to continue his father's legacy as a successful entrepreneur. His educational pedigree and business training further validated his place among the black elite. He returned to Memphis with high expectations from his family and the city. "In the natural course of time he will succeed his worthy sire as the wealthiest colored man in America," predicted G. P. Hamilton in 1908. He placed his political aspiration largely on hold to appease his father. Within three short years after returning to the Bluff City, he had established himself as "a veritable chip off the old block" and began to carve out his own legacy.[24]

Just prior to his return to Memphis, Church rekindled a friendship with a young lady he had known since childhood, Sara (Sallie) Parodi Johnson. The two presumably met during one of Robert's many visits to Washington, D.C., as a child. They reunited in New York, and Robert wrote Sallie often. In a 1909 letter from Mary she thanked Robert for a great time in New York and sent "love and kisses" from herself, "Mama Lou" (Louisa Ayers Church—Church Senior's first wife), and "a certain young teacher."[25] Sallie belonged to a well-known African American family in Washington, D.C., and attended the most famous black high school in the country, M Street High. She served as vice president of her class. After graduating in 1903, Sallie enrolled at Myrtilla Miner Normal School (now the University of the District of Columbia). The Myrtilla Miner Normal School initially designed its curriculum to train African American women to become teachers. It later expanded its mission to also training black men. Many of its graduates, including Sallie, received priority to fill the District's teaching vacancies.[26]

Sallie taught in Washington until she married Church on July 26, 1911, at the Fifteenth Street Presbyterian Church in Washington, D.C. Francis James Grimké, renowned activist and minister, served as the ceremony's officiant. The month following the extravaganza, black intellectual W. E. B. Du Bois wrote Robert and Sallie to congratulate them "on the commencement of their new life." The future looked bright for Church and his bride as the two newlyweds returned to Memphis days later, anxious to embark on their new lives together. He only regretted that his parents could not attend the wedding. His father's health was declining, and his mother stayed in Memphis to tend to her ill husband. By the following summer, his father and hero had passed away. At the time of his death on August 29, 1912, Church Senior had amassed a fortune reputed to be valued at more than $1,000,000.[27]

# Coming of Age

I N THE WAKE OF THE DEATH of Robert R. Church Sr., condolence letters poured in from across the country. Journalist and antilynching advocate Ida B. Wells-Barnett expressed her sympathies to the younger Church and the family. "Although I had heard he was ill, yet I had hoped for the pleasure of once more meeting him in life," expressed Wells. She continued, "I rejoice exceedingly that he has so worthy a son to take up the work and carry it on now on his own responsibility. . . . May you like Solomon be given wisdom with which to fulfill your trust to the honor of your race and your generation."[1] For his entire life Robert walked in the shadow of a giant, and suddenly the family looked to him to fill his father's void. He received other letters that encouraged him to protect his family's legacy in the city. Booker T. Washington challenged Church to "continue to enrich our race through your efforts."[2] Church Junior, a southern gentleman educated at the finest schools, and the son of a wealthy businessman, found himself at a crossroads both personally and professionally.[3]

As condolences continued to pour in, the Churches began to execute Church Senior's last will and testament. He named Anna the sole executrix of his will and bequeathed unto her approximately twenty-five properties he owned in Memphis, as well as Chicago and Washington, D.C. He left his son a watch, chain, and diamond stud. Although Anna officially served as the heir to his fortune, Church Junior managed the bulk of the family's estate. Thomas and Mary, products of his first marriage, to Louisa Ayers, shared an additional forty-five properties in Shelby County.

As the family grieved and attempted to move forward with divvying up the properties, a skeleton from their father's past revealed itself. A young woman from Vancouver, British Columbia, by the name of Laura Church Napier claimed to be the daughter of the real estate mogul and contested the will. In her statement to the court she claimed that Church Senior "always recognized her as his daughter." Laura was born prior to the Civil War in New Orleans, making her the oldest of the other four children he raised in Memphis. Church had a serious relationship with a woman by the name of Margaret Pico in New Orleans during his time as a steward on his father's steamboats. According to the *Chicago Defender*, a staff correspondent in New Orleans found several records from long before the Civil War in a safety-deposit vault including an aged and tattered marriage certificate between the two. According to the records, Church afforded her opportunities similar to his other four children. Laura attended private schools and eventually graduated from Fisk University in Nashville. The *Chicago Defender* claimed, "it is known by a great many that Mrs. Napier lived with the family in Memphis ever since [Mr.] Church's marriage to the present widow, formerly Miss Anna Wright of Memphis."[4] There is no evidence that the children refuted any claims that she was their half-sister, but they did stage a united front to prevent Napier from receiving any of their father's assets. Laura believed that she, too, should benefit from her father's estate and subsequently filed a lawsuit in Shelby County's Probate Court.[5]

Church acted on behalf of the family and hired the highly successful Memphis attorneys S. M. Neely and former governor of Tennessee Malcolm R. Patterson. The case continued for three years until the Tennessee Supreme Court upheld the decision that Church's will could not be attacked and Laura Napier had no standing in court.[6]

The Churches' reaction may have been motivated primarily by financial gain, but it also revealed a larger concern they had with protecting their family's image and legacy. The Churches needed to appear as an ideal family. Their father certainly deserved to be remembered for his pioneering accomplishments, but he was no saint. He could be an unforgiving person with a volatile temper, at times unapproachable. He built a great deal of his fortune with the saloons he owned on Beale Street, where at times he would be arrested for violent confrontations with his patrons and the police. Church and his siblings went to great lengths to protect the sanctity of the Church family name, even if it meant romanticizing their past. In this defense of his father, Church Junior emerged as the family patriarch. He remained committed to upholding the legacy of his namesake.

His father's death also marks a transitional period in Church's life as he attempted to expand his influence in the Bluff City.[7]

Throughout the ordeal, Church continued to serve as president of the Solvent Savings Bank, even though he worked primarily as a real estate operator. The money and properties he managed allowed him the financial freedom to pursue politics. The political arena is where Church exceeded his father's notoriety on the national scene. He served as a lifelong member of the Republican Party, but his affiliation with the GOP moved beyond blindly campaigning for its candidates. He understood the limitations of the party, as well as its leaders. However, Church felt that the Republican Party presented him with the best opportunity to demonstrate the political agency of African Americans in the South specifically, but nationally as well. In his eyes the "Party of Lincoln" represented more than a political organization; it represented more so the neglect of Lincoln's political successors toward black society, as well as the most pragmatic approach to improving the lives of African Americans. Racism existed in both political parties, and Robert believed that African Americans could not expect much, in terms of racial progress, from Democrats or lily-white Republicans. Therefore he pressured the Republican Party to remain true to what he perceived as the promise of Lincoln.[8]

Church did not have a seamless transition from the business sector to the political arena. After returning from New York, he attempted to make a name for himself in his hometown as a political figure, and apparently made some disparaging comments about women's suffrage. It caught the attention of his sister. Mary Church Terrell scolded her younger brother about his sexist stance. "My dear little Baby Brother," Terrell wrote, "you say you don't believe in woman suffrage. You just mean to say you have never thought seriously on this subject." She stated that she would have confronted him earlier, but she feared that he "may never write again." Terrell told her brother, twenty years her junior, to reconsider his stance and to "think about it seriously from every point of view," and that "surely you believe I am as capable of discharging the duties and obligations of citizenship" as any man. "No colored man who believes in suffrage for colored men can consistently oppose it. Unless you believe all men who are born colored, should because of that accident of race be deprived of the right of citizenship, you cannot insist that all human beings who are born girls should because of that accident of sex be denied rights which others enjoy simply because they happened to be born boys," wrote Terrell.[9]

Her stance on race and gender echoed the sentiments she expressed over a decade earlier in her address to the National American Woman Suffrage Association (NAWSA), of which she was a life member. She was offended by the position he had taken and told him she had a letter on women's suffrage with her that she had written when she was fifteen years old, and assured him that she was indeed "an old soldier in the cause 'sho-nuff.'" She concluded by telling him to kiss the new bride and signed it "Your affectionate sister."[10] Church had to reflect on the stern comments made by his sister, for whom he had deep admiration. Terrell forced Church to reconsider this strategy by proving the hypocrisy of his stance. Whether willingly or regretfully, Church heeded his sister's advice and began to re-think his position on women's suffrage.[11]

As Church matured as a leader, he took a more sophisticated approach to politics. In 1912, torn between his duties as president of the bank and his desire to enter politics full-time, he decided to resign his position. He left the institution that his father founded because it did not fit his vision of leadership. His father believed that the Solvent Savings Bank promoted thrift among the black masses, and he believed in the promise of economic uplift. The bank provided loans to black entrepreneurs who could not obtain funding from the predominantly white banks in the city. This offered an alternative for the city's black residents to invest their money without the threat of being swindled by the high interest rates offered by its white competitors. Church initially embraced his father's ideas about educating the masses about fiscal responsibility and the idea that economic security would help sustain a strong, self-sufficient black community in Memphis. This in turn would grant black Memphians the financial freedom to challenge white supremacy through various forms of activism. The bank eventually became the center of the black business district on Beale Street. However, Church needed a new challenge.[12]

At the time of Church's resignation, the Solvent Savings Bank and Trust Company sold shares of stock at $10. It had deposits of approximately $90,000 and over $10,000 in capital. The bank thrived for decades, having more than $1,000,000 deposited by 1920. Although Beale Street gained a reputation for being the mecca for black capitalism in the Mid-South, Church understood that his and his colleagues' successes did not represent the nearly fifty-two thousand African Americans living in Memphis. The overwhelming majority of black Memphians remained poor and did not have money to invest in the bank. The average black person worked in unskilled positions and struggled to make ends meet. Most had little money to deposit in a bank or to pursue lucrative business ventures. However, Church did believe that everyone, regardless of class, could participate in the political process. Although the average black resident did not benefit directly from the bank, Church convinced many of his father's former business associates to form the "nucleus for the potent, political bloc" he envisioned.[13] This allowed Church to redirect his energy from the private sector to advocating for political rights on behalf of all black Americans.[14]

Church began his political crusade in his hometown, gradually increasing his presence on the national stage. To have a serious presence in Memphis politics, Church first needed to build a relationship with the city's notorious political boss, Edward Hull Crump. The "Crump Machine" dominated the local political scene throughout the first half of the twentieth century. The supposedly progressive agenda of Crump often neglected the needs of the black community. "His progressivism was that of business efficiency and corporate regulation, not social justice," wrote historian Lester Lamon.[15] Therefore, Church worked with prominent black Memphians Bert M. Roddy and Harry H. Pace, both high-ranking officials in the Solvent Savings Bank and personal friends of his father, to form the Colored Citizens Association (CCA). In 1911, the CCA organized a successful voter-registration drive in the black community, garnering the attention of Crump and his opponent. The CCA strategically negotiated a deal with Crump that included the needs of the African Americans in the reforms he promised. They placed an emphasis on improving their neighborhoods, asking specifically for new parks and paved roads. At a CCA meeting, Pace pleaded to vote for Crump because "the other candidate promises everything and I fear he will do nothing; but this redheaded fellow frankly declines to promise some of the things we want, but convinced me that he will fulfill the promises that he did make."[16] Crump won the election and in 1913 opened the all-black Douglass Park. He also authorized other improvements in the black community.[17]

This was the beginning of a thirty-year political relationship. Both Church and Crump were regarded as the "bosses" of their respective political factions. Church could deliver the black vote in West Tennessee, and Crump ruled the local political scene in Memphis. For these two political giants to coexist in the city, they realized they would have to work with each other. African Americans could vote if they paid the poll tax required by the Tennessee Constitution. Crump understood that those voters could not be ignored and were vital to the success of his political machine. Church, for his part, knew it was highly unlikely for a Republican candidate to win a local election, especially since African Americans were still outnumbered in Shelby County. Instead he used his appeal in the black community to force Crump to consider some of the demands made by black Memphians. Church also knew that, for African Americans to maintain their right to vote in the state, they needed to ally themselves with the city's most powerful politician. He conveyed to his constituents that, even though they voted for Democrats locally, their loyalty remained with the Republicans, and they could still vote for the GOP in national elections. The strategy Church employed allowed him to increase his influence in the state and organize a substantial political bloc that had to be reckoned with throughout the state.[18]

This relationship with Crump during the 1911 mayoral campaign established Church as a master organizer and a respected leader among black Memphians. He could align the black vote with the candidate(s) who could deliver the most rewards for their communities.[19] This set the stage for his political aspirations during the upcoming national elections the following year.

Church recognized the political agency that black Tennesseans possessed compared to other southern states. Tennessee's voting requirements did not resemble some of the other more extreme Jim Crow measures exhibited throughout the South. Besides the state-imposed poll-tax requirement, there was no statewide white-primary rule, which made it difficult to prevent African Americans from voting. According to political scientist Paul Lewinson, "every vote counted" in Memphis.[20] Church's ability to secure this large voting bloc raised the awareness of factional leaders in both parties. Although Republicans coveted the black vote, the party's lily-white faction attempted to prohibit black membership. Robert met this challenge head-on.[21]

Most accounts of Church inaccurately characterize him as a person who solely delivered black votes for Republican candidates. However, the significance of Church's lifelong political crusade can be best gleaned in his fight against the lily-whites. He is often remembered as one of the party's most loyal black supporters, but Church was also one of its most vocal critics. The lily-white movement surfaced during Reconstruction as a response to assertions made by southern Democrats who considered their Republican counterparts "nigger lovers." Therefore, the lily-whites made a concerted effort "to take control of the Republican organizations in the South into their white hands."[22] The Democrats had already effectively built a reputation as the "white man's" party, and Republicans set out to accomplish the same. White Republicans feared that black men would dominate the party in the South. The creation of the lily-white faction thus transcended politics; it embodied the southern culture of segregation. According to Hanes Walton Jr., the construction of the faction was inevitable. The space that white supremacy created also provided a counter space for Robert Church Jr. to develop a parallel organization, and ultimately his own political machine as a response to southern segregationists. Robert would later align himself with the interracial faction composed of black Republicans and sympathetic whites known as the "black-and-tans." This interracial coalition provided Church with the necessary leverage to establish his faction as the more powerful Republicans in the county.[23]

In 1912, Church made his first of eight successful bids to represent the Tenth District of Memphis at the Republican National Convention. In response to his election, the lily-white Shelby County Republican organization tried to prevent him from attending the convention. This brought a local battle to the national stage. But Church led his Tennessee group of "black-and-tans" to the convention and demanded to be seated. He benefited from the "numerical superiority of blacks in the party in Shelby County,"[24] and he supported President William Howard Taft's reelection. Taft controlled the convention that year, and his faction rejected the bid of the lily-whites because they were considered "Roosevelt men."[25] Church kept his seat at the convention and in turn worked hard to campaign for Taft. Although the Republicans were soundly defeated by Woodrow Wilson, making him the first Democrat to win office since Grover Cleveland in 1892, Church had his baptism in national politics.

As Church's notoriety grew, so did his roles within the family. On his twenty-eighth birthday his mother, Anna, wished him a life of "happiness and success" and told him to continue enriching the lives of the people he touched and to continue to "comfort your family." In the spirit of her deceased husband, she also wished that he would grow and "be a stronger and better man each day."[26] Anna Church frequently wrote her son to acknowledge his various accomplishments. He also remained very close to his sister Annette, but he longed for a family of his own. In 1915, Robert and Sallie welcomed their first and only child, Sara Roberta Church.

Known as Roberta, she was born in Washington, D.C., at the home of Sallie's mother. Roberta attended the private schools in Memphis and later graduated from Lemoyne High. Roberta went on to receive her bachelor's and master's degrees from Northwestern University in sociology and psychology, respectively. She later followed in her father's footsteps and became an important presence within the Republican Party. During the 1950s, President Dwight Eisenhower made Roberta the highest-ranking African American female appointee in his administration.[27]

After his daughter's birth, Church focused on developing a strategy that would increase the presence of African Americans within the GOP. He needed an agenda that stimulated the interest of black voters and convinced them to take a more substantial role in politics. Church needed to develop a plan to pay poll taxes for those who could not afford it. Church would use small venues, mainly the Church Auditorium, as meeting places to inform black voters about the political process. He wanted to create a more politically sophisticated black voting constituency in Memphis. Although this seemed to be a daunting task, Church exuded confidence and invested a considerable amount of financial and intellectual capital into this movement. A journalist described Church as "conservative by nature. But when he is right, he is very persistent and cannot be frightened from his course."[28] He wanted "the united support of his race." Independently wealthy, Church did not participate in politics for financial gain or popularity. In fact, he often avoided the limelight and appointed other qualified leaders to be the face of various issues. Church emphasized developing an organization that displayed the collective strength of the black community, and granted everyone, regardless of class or gender, the opportunity to participate in the political process.[29]

Church turned to a group of established leaders and professionals who had influence beyond the Bluff City. Church met with prominent black Memphians Thomas Hayes, Wayman Wilkerson, Levi McCoy, Josiah Settle Jr., and Bert Roddy and formed the Lincoln Republican Club. It later became known as the Lincoln Republican League of Tennessee. These men had equal stature to Church, and the majority of them had worked with his father. They offered insightful feedback and had the credibility to critique Church's decisions if necessary. He purposefully avoided leaders he could dominate or easily influence. A local newspaper complimented Church for how he assembled his team of advisors. The article stated, "in the past, far too often, when a strong character in the Negro race has sought to launch an enterprise, he has surrounded himself with weaklings, perhaps thinking that he might shine the brighter as a brilliant star, if surrounded by far dimmer stars only." It continued, "The men launching the Lincoln Republican Club took pains to put several bright stars together."[30] These members of the black elite had the daunting task of developing an organization that would speak to, speak for, and speak with the black masses in West Tennessee.[31]

Political scientist Melissa Harris-Perry (Lacewell) argues that members of the black elite spoke to black people "to frame the solutions to the black dilemma." They spoke for the black community "when they are under the gaze of white power structures that attempt to understand and predict, what the Negro wants from the appeals of leaders." Furthermore, "they speak with black people in an intricate, reciprocal cultural reproduction of ideas."[32] The Lincoln League's success depended on the cooperation of the entire community. Church and the other officers articulated the aims of the organization and explained how they planned to integrate the leadership within the Republican Party. Church established connections with influential whites and blacks throughout the country and planned to produce a platform that addressed the issues most pertinent to all African Americans. The Lincoln League embodied the collective strength of the black community and called on all its citizens to be active agents in the organization by encouraging them to offer solutions to their common problems.[33]

The Lincoln League provides a model for understanding the dynamics of black leadership in the early twentieth century. Scholars have criticized the efforts of the black elite as disingenuous or labeled the elites as opportunists. While some of these criticisms are warranted, the black working class held Church and his peers in esteem. African Americans have traditionally rallied to support defiant individuals who refused to succumb to white supremacy, and the black community respected leaders who embodied the tradition of defiance that has historically fueled black freedom struggles. Therefore, black Memphians supported Church not because of his wealth and family pedigree, but because he created an opportunity for all African Americans in the city to "retain a sense of selfhood in the face of constant subordination and dehumanization in the American system."[34]

On the evening of February 1, 1916, Church and over one thousand potential voters gathered at Church Park on Beale Street. A local black newspaper reported, "Remember the date for in all likelihood it is to become historic."[35] In a letter written to his close friend and prominent black Republican leader Roscoe Conkling Simmons, Church described the evening as a "very bitter [cold] night," but the event was filled with enthusiasm.[36] He asked Simmons, a newspaper editor and master orator, to produce a story that could be sent to the leading colored papers in town. In a pamphlet, presumably written by Simmons, the leaders outlined the goals of the organization. They proclaimed that the Lincoln League intended to teach African Americans the "higher art of politics." Acknowledging the influence of Jim Crow, the message stated, "Call it a move of segregation, if you will, but the cold fact remains: the colored voter must either vote as a unit or continue to be politically expunged as at present."[37] Church called for members to follow the principles of the organization and not the men. This approach would preserve the organization regardless of its leaders. The Lincoln League also made it clear the only qualifications for membership were that a person must be a qualified voter and sign or endorse the constitution of the Lincoln Republican League. Church later declared that the Lincoln League "is distinctly founded for the good of the masses and not the classes of men."[38] Church Park and Auditorium served as its headquarters. Members elected Church as the president of the organization and Thomas Hayes, Wayman Wilkerson, Levi McCoy, Josiah Settle Jr., and Bert M. Roddy as its officers. For the first time, blacks in Memphis had a viable organization to offer a serious threat to the lily-white Shelby County Republican Organization during the upcoming election.[39]

The Lincoln League also functioned as an instrument for social and educational change. The organization provided an opportunity for black Memphians to congregate and discuss issues, such as lynching, women's suffrage, and blacks in the military. Perhaps the league's greatest contribution other than its political achievements was in education. Church helped to establish numerous voter schools throughout the county. He financed practically the entire venture out of his own pocket. The academies taught the fundamentals of voting, but more importantly it taught the city's black residents the fundamentals of reading. At the turn of the century a sizeable portion of the city's black residents remained illiterate. Although Tennessee had not instituted literacy tests as a voting requirement, Church and the other officers wanted to be certain that their members did not accidentally vote against the candidates supported by the Lincoln League. Church also speculated that Tennessee would join other southern states and enact literacy and property requirements at its fall state constitutional convention, effectively ending what many considered the most liberal franchise in the South.

The burden of improving literacy in the black community fell largely on the women. Although they could not officially hold membership in the league because at the time they did not qualify as "eligible voters," they were essential to its success due to their role primarily as teachers in the voting academies.[40] Women regularly attended the meetings, as suggested by photographs, and understood the aims of the organization.

The teachers of the voting schools used various instructional methods and held class nightly at Church Auditorium. Church explained the teaching process in a letter he wrote to a master's student at Tennessee Agricultural & Industrial State University. For literate voters, teachers used ballots to demonstrate the methods used at the ballot box. The instructors urged them to vote the straight Republican ticket and avoid simple mistakes. For illiterate voters, teachers taught them basic reading skills so they could vote for the Republican candidates. Others were taught to "single shot" the ballot by voting for the Republican candidate for governor and ignoring the other races. Church believed this to be the most effective method because black voters would often vote for more than one candidate for the same office and invalidate their ballots.[41]

The local newspaper, the *Commercial Appeal,* became intrigued by the activity of the Lincoln League. It employed several black and white men to infiltrate the organization and report its findings. The newspaper reported on October 22, 1916, that Church and other officers funded the efforts of the organization, and received funds from the National Republican Headquarters. It also confirmed that the league's presence extended beyond the Tenth District and influenced voters throughout West Tennessee. Finally, it correctly concluded that the League used women to serve as instructors for the voting academies and hinted that these women were "well paid." Despite efforts to rally white Memphians to obstruct the success of the Lincoln League, Church continued the movement.[42]

The Lincoln League worked diligently to register voters in the city. In the spring of 1916 the league issued a letter signed by Church, Walter L.

Cohen, and Roscoe Conkling Simmons. It charged: "The defense of our people must come from us, and not from others. The time to step out is today and not tomorrow. The infamy of the political conspiracy which looks to the political slavery of our children we will meet as men and we will call to our aid those whom we have lifted by our ballots and see if the constitution is strong enough to hold up the common citizenship of this country."[43]

Thousands of black Memphians responded to this charge. The party received an additional boost after Robert was elected as a delegate at large for the upcoming Republican National Convention in June. He became the first black Tennessean since 1892 to hold this distinction. The *Nashville Globe* reported, "The Negroes of Tennessee ought to get squarely behind.... No one will deny the fact that the white Republican is trying with vehemence to rid himself of the black as a factor in conventions, while at the same time courting the Negroes assiduously along about election time. Mr. Church and his numerous followers are going to carry the war right up to the National Convention."[44] The lily-whites from Tennessee predictably challenged his nomination. Church urged Roscoe Simmons to have him issue a statement to prominent members of the national organization informing them that "in Shelby county alone there are more than 10,000 colored voters who could be controlled by the Republican organization if the men who could whip this vote in line were given some recognition." He assured the politicians, "I have no personal or selfish motive that is prompting me to make this fight, but my friends have insisted that since I have been doing some special work for the National leaders for the past year, that I can best make the fight. However, that is secondary, I only want to see the Tenth Congressional district represented by a colored delegate, since there is but one, instead of a white delegate."[45] The national committee agreed. Despite opposition from lily-whites, Robert attended the convention in June and returned to Memphis to prepare for the presidential and gubernatorial elections. That summer the national organization also named him a member of the Advisory Committee for Negroes to aid its national campaign committee. Church's individual status within the Party of Lincoln continued to rise as he strengthened the movement in Memphis.[46]

By October 1916 the Lincoln League successfully registered 10,612 African Americans, accounting for nearly one-third of the total 32,348 registered voters in Shelby County. The league held a meeting on September 8 and adopted the platform for the Lincoln Republican League Ticket. This separate Republican ticket posed a direct challenge to the Shelby County Republicans. Wayman Wilkerson, the Lincoln League's candidate for Congress, and "the arch lily-whitist" John W. Farley headlined the election. Church told Roscoe Simmons that he hoped their ticket "will run 3,000 votes ahead of this one." Church most wanted to annihilate the lily-whites to prove that a Republican candidate would never win office in the city or state without reconsidering its segregationist position.[47]

The platform of the Lincoln League ticket articulated the issues most pertinent to the black community. It supported labor unions for the "mutual protection" of "working men and working women," the abolition of Jim Crow government in the South, antilynching legislation, and equal rights for black soldiers in the military. The platform also emphasized the need to pass legislation to address the inadequacy and inequity of education for African Americans, and to allow the "immediate extension of the vote to women." Church, who helped to draft the platform, learned from the conversations with his sister Mary. The platform included the language: "The right to vote is a right inherent in every American citizen, and any abridgement thereof is a perversion of the organic law both in letter and spirit." It continued: "The claim that the right to vote should not be withheld from those able to bear arms in defense of the country involves no stronger reason than the claim that universal suffrage ought to be extended to those who bear the children that make the soldiers of tomorrow, and to all women who so nobly bear the common burdens of the republic. We believe in both the equality of sexes and the equality of men. The members of the Lincoln League made it clear that "we favor the immediate extension of the vote to women."[48] The platform also announced its candidates for office, most notable Wayman Wilkerson for Congress, Bert Roddy and H. M. Bomar for state senators, and Thomas H. Hayes for floterial senator. The members of the Lincoln League adopted the platform without a dissenting vote. Church considered the meeting a great success. The Lincoln League carried the momentum into November as they prepared to confront their lily-white counterparts.

In Church's final address, just a few days prior to the election, he once again stated that the objective of the Lincoln League was to promote the principles of the Republican Party and protect the interest of African

American voters in Tennessee.[49] He explained his intentions of making the league an invaluable asset to the GOP in the state and the nation, and reminded them they had a reasonable chance to elect an African American to the U.S. Senate and as governor of Tennessee.

On the morning of the election, the *Commercial Appeal* countered Church's plea with a display of racist "yellow" journalism. The article urged white Democrats to go to the polls and claimed that blacks and whites were attempting "to herd the ignorant Negro voters to the poll today" and split the white Democratic vote in the city. "There are 10,612 Negroes registered in Shelby County. There are just 21,636 white registered in Shelby County. Every black vote counts Presidential year. Suppose the white vote is split? Go to the polls today. Vote for Woodrow Wilson and the straight Democratic ticket and write the brand of shame across the hideous plot." The *Commercial Appeal* spread fear of a black political takeover. The newspaper already served as the unofficial organ of white supremacy in Memphis, with outlandish stories of black men as rapists and its daily stereotypical political cartoon, "Hambone's Meditations." White Democrats responded to the call and swept the elections that year.[50]

Although the loss could be considered a political failure based on the overall outcome of the election, Church still viewed the election as an overwhelming success. He knew the unlikelihood of defeating the Democrats and Boss Crump's political machine. Instead he intended for his movement to obstruct the growth of the lily-whites in Tennessee and the entire southern region. In this regard, he succeeded as the Lincoln League candidates outpolled the lily-white Republicans nearly four to one, leading Church to declare that the Lincoln League ticket represented the "Regular Republicans" in Tennessee. *Champion Magazine*, based out of Chicago, declared, "In our opinion it was the most significant phase of the recent election." The article made clear that the Lincoln League did not work to promote any individual politician, or establish "Negro supremacy." Instead it worked "to regain the lost rights of a growing race." It concluded, "We congratulate the Colored people of Tennessee upon the success of their Lincoln League and their Robert Church."[51] Other national newspapers applauded their efforts to challenge the lily-white wing of the party who, much like the Democrats, intended to keep African Americans politically powerless.

Church's success in organizing the Lincoln League, combined with his ability to secure the black vote in Memphis, caught the attention of

Republicans in Washington, D.C. He had finally emerged from the shadow of his father and began to receive praise based on his own merit. In the subsequent years, Church transitioned from a local leader to a national figure. During the various campaigns, he built relationships with other prominent leaders, both white and black. They all coveted his expertise and attempted to align themselves with the rising star. Church had matured as a leader, and he hoped to empower all black Americans with his message of political uplift.

# The Roving Dictator of the Lincoln Belt

"MEMPHIS PRESENTED A STRANGE PARADOX," wrote Gerald Capers, "a city modern in physical aspect but rural in background, rural in prejudice, and rural in habit."[1] By the World War I era the city boasted at least three colleges, a medical school, six hospitals, and three business colleges. Automobiles, paved streets, buildings, and city parks reflected the city's urban landscape. Aesthetically, Memphis seemed to be amid an urban renaissance. It also appeared to be a possible haven for rural blacks who wanted to escape the hostile environment of the Mississippi Delta. It was the only place in the region that had a substantial black professional class, and because of the work of Church and others, black Memphians had a political voice in a southern city. Beale Street had been transformed from a once posh exclusively white residential area into the "Main Street of Negro America."[2] On Beale you could find everything from the offices of the leading black professionals in the city to banks, auditoriums, music clubs, saloons, gambling dens, and restaurants. Musicians such as W. C. Handy, "Father of the Blues," helped to introduce a new musical genre to America. Memphis emerged as an attractive alternative to mundane country life. With a sprawling downtown, a prominent skyline, new industries, a politically conscious black community, and a "progressive" mayor, Memphis in many ways epitomized the promise of a modern southern city.[3]

Despite the city's physical improvement, its culture reflected the traditions and ideology of its rural neighbors. White Memphians remained resistant to social change. Many had migrated from the Delta and brought with them their own system of values and beliefs. Religion in particular had an enormous effect on the southern way of life. H. L. Mencken deemed Memphis "the Buckle of the Bible Belt," referencing the unique form of evangelical Protestantism that permeated the area. Their religion led some white Memphians to reject certain characteristics associated with urban life, viewing them as a threat to their southern traditions. They were consumed with their concepts of honor and "right to vengeance," and considered it their sacred duty to protect their women and children from the moral and racial corruption of urban America.

Black progress posed a threat to the racial hierarchy of the South. So aside from defending the sanctity of their women, they felt equally passionate about maintaining their political autonomy. As Amy Wood wrote, white southerners "conceptualized the threat of black enfranchisement and autonomy as, above all, a dire moral threat to white purity, literally a physical assault on white homes and white women."[4]

By 1916, Church had successfully mobilized the black vote in Memphis and established himself as the preeminent black political leader in Tennessee. His political victories cemented his position as a leader in the community, but also posed a serious threat to the fundamental beliefs of white supremacists. This created an intense racial climate in the city. Black political participation is inherently tied to some of the egregious forms of racial violence in American history. It functions as a powder keg for vigilante violence, where an already dangerous atmosphere is merely waiting for a spark. That spark came in the spring of 1917, when a black woodchopper was lynched in the city. At that moment, Church witnessed the extent to which white Memphians would go to protect their racial hegemony in the area.

On Wednesday, May 2, 1917, a white sixteen-year-old schoolgirl named Antoinette Rappel was brutally raped and murdered near the Wolf River Bridge on the outskirts of Memphis. Her decapitated corpse was found "lying on its back, with arms and limbs outstretched, and with clothing torn and disheveled."[5] That day the Memphis dailies suggested that a black man had attacked her and vigilante justice should be served. The *News Scimitar* reported "that every indication tends to fasten the crime to a negro wood cutter, or more likely two of them."[6] The *Commercial Appeal* explained Rappel's decapitated state by planting the idea that "a large number of Negroes worked as wood cutters in the area."[7] This image captured the imagination of white Memphians. The reports served as a rallying cry for white men to reassert their dominance. Most importantly, the Rappel murder provided an opportunity for white Memphians to reclaim their city not only from what they perceived as black sexual predators, but also from leaders like Church who threatened the tenets of southern culture.[8]

Shelby County Sheriff Mike Tate led the investigation of the murder. The initial evidence suggested that a white male had committed the crime. Detectives Charles Brunner and John Boyle found Rappel's bicycle standing against a tree with the contents inside her basket undisturbed, implying that she may have known her attacker. Also, her assailant left a white jacket and handkerchief at the scene of the crime, attire not typically associated with the poor woodcutters in the area. Dr. Lee A Stone commented, "It is practically a certainty . . . that this terrible crime has been committed by a white man."[9] Instead of Tate following the leads of detectives Brunner and Boyle, he chose to rely on the testimony of an African American deaf mute by the name of Dewitt Ford. Ford worked as a woodcutter near the scene of the murder and reenacted the attack through an elaborate performance that involved a series of physical gestures and grimaces. Ford, also known as "Dummy" by his employer, allegedly stood behind a tree and witnessed the murder. Subsequently, several suspects were brought in for questioning without any success. Finally, Tate turned to a thirty-something black woodcutter by the name of Ell Persons. He had previously interrogated and released Persons on two separate occasions. Frustrated with false leads and the increasing pressure from the white community to find Rappel's killer, Tate, in an act of desperation, followed the advice of a New York criminologist and photographed the eye of the deceased girl. According to the French scientist Alphonse Bertillion, a person's retina retained the image of his/her killer. Officer Paul Waggener photographed Rappel's left eye because her right eye had decomposed. He claimed he could see the forehead and hair of Ell Persons.[10]

On May 8, 1917, a grand jury indicted Ell Persons. He was immediately taken to Nashville for his own protection as he awaited trial. On May 21, as he traveled back to Memphis for a court date, a mob took Persons from two police officers without any struggle. They immediately began to plan his murder. The *Commercial Appeal* and *News-Scimitar* advertised the location and time of the proposed lynching. The *Commercial Appeal* ran the headline, "mob captures slayer of the rappel girl: Ell Persons to Be Lynched Near Scene of Murder, May Resort to Burning." An estimated 2,000–4,000 men waited at the Wolf River Bridge on the night of his abduction. That number increased to around 6,000 men, women, and children the following morning. The atmosphere resembled a festival more than a public execution. People acted as police officers and directed traffic. Vendors had concession stands and sold drinks, peanuts, cotton candy, and ice cream to the anxious onlookers.[11]

The proceedings began around 9:00 a.m. In the presence of thousands of spectators, Persons confessed to the crime. A local pastor was summoned to allow Persons to pray in accordance with the lynching ritual. However, a spectator countered that Persons did not allow Rappel to pray before she died. The victim's mother, Minnie Woods yelled, "Don't shoot him, please. . . . I want him to suffer 10,000 times more than did my little girl. Burn him, Burn him!" The mob respected her wishes and led Persons to a pit filled with tree branches soaked in gasoline. The vigilantes then drenched Persons in gasoline, alcohol, and kerosene and proceeded to burn him alive.[12]

With his body ablaze, the crowd sang "John Brown's Body" and "My Old Kentucky Home." After the fire burned out and with his body smoldering from the ritualistic sacrifice, the crowd rushed his body to gather souvenirs from his charred corpse. They cut off his ears, nose, lips, and fingers. Finally someone decapitated Persons in the same manner as Rappel. His severed head was then thrown onto Beale Street, not far from the offices of Church and the city's other leading black businessmen. The actions of the mob made it clear that they wanted to do more than terrorize the person suspected of the crime. They also wanted Church and his peers to understand the lengths whites would go to to protect the racial hierarchy of the Bluff City.[13]

Historian W. Fitzhugh Brundage describes mass lynch mobs as numbering between fifty and several thousand people, with the full support of their community for extralegal and illegal activities. Brundage states that mass mobs demonstrated the "highly ritualized choreography" of the chase, the selection of a sacrificial site, the sadistic torture and burning of the victim, and the collection of mementos from the victim's body. This type of community-sanctioned violence reflected the culture of the South and symbolized the atmosphere in which Church operated.[14]

It is also fair to criticize the city's black leaders. The Ell Persons lynching not only exposes how white supremacists viewed African Americans, but also shows how African American viewed themselves. Class and group affiliation shared the activism in the city. Church and other members of the black elite did nothing to prevent the lynching of Ell Persons. In fact, as historians Kenneth Goings and Gerald Smith highlight, no "community" came to his defense, perhaps because Persons did not belong to any defined group. He was not a member of the black professional class or the larger working class in Memphis. Instead Persons "was an itinerant woodchopper, a migrant to the area who lived a relatively isolated existence in a woods outside of Memphis." The city had a history of black activism, but for the most part these activists geared their efforts toward members of a specific group. The Persons lynching revealed a fundamental flaw in the black elite's racial uplift strategy. As Goings and Smith state, the Talented Tenth in the city sought racial redress through legal and political action. Accommodationists were not willing to jeopardize their lives because it would do nothing to "foster harmonious race relations."[15] However, the actions of the mob suggest that, despite Church's distance from people like Persons, whites tended to view all African Americans, despite class, in a similar light.

By throwing Persons's head onto Beale Street, the mob posed a direct challenge to black success. Church responded by becoming a more vocal critic of lynching. The lynching transformed black activism in the city, as Church and his allies attempted to align themselves with larger organizations and institutions that had the resources to expose these southern traditions on an international stage. Much like when his father was shot during the 1866 riots, Church became a victim of racial violence. Although he did not suffer any physical injury, it became clear that the white community perceived him as an enemy. Unlike his father, the younger Church was not as willing to accommodate the demands of the white community. He was more expressive in his disapproval for these heinous crimes.[16]

Within days of the lynching, Church met with his longtime friend since his days on Wall Street, James Weldon Johnson. On the day Johnson arrived, Church drove him to the lynching site. Johnson recalled, "A pile of ashes and pieces of charred wood still marked the spot." After envisioning the scene, Johnson stated, "I tried to balance the sufferings of the miserable victim against the moral degradation of Memphis, and the truth flashed over me that in large measure the race question involves the saving of black America's body and white America's soul."[17] Church served as host and guide for the next ten days as Johnson investigated the murder. Johnson interviewed Sheriff Tate, black and white residents, and newspaper reporters. He published his findings in *The Crisis*.[18]

Johnson found that Memphis's black community wanted to enlist the help of the National Association for the Advancement of Colored People (NAACP). Black Memphians were still excited about what they accomplished the previous year with the Lincoln League. League member Bert Roddy had worked since 1914 to establish an NAACP branch in Memphis after attending a meeting hosted by the organization's board chairman, Joel Spingarn, and W. E. B. Du Bois. Johnson met with Roddy and Church to discuss the necessary steps for establishing a branch in Memphis. On June 11, 1917, prior to Johnson's departure, Church provided the names and membership dues of fifty-three potential members, including himself; his wife, Sallie; his mother, Anna; and his sister Annette. The Church women were the only women who signed the charter. Although members only needed to submit one dollar to be considered active, over one-third of the applicants donated the maximum of five dollars. They impressed the national headquarters with their commitment, and the NAACP granted a charter to Memphis on June 26. They secured a permanent charter the following year. Bert Roddy served as the branch's first president, and Church served as the chairman of the Executive Committee.[19]

The Memphis branch played an integral role in expanding the NAACP's presence in the South. However, not everyone was willing to remain in an area where nearly 10,000 people witnessed a lynching and no one was arrested. The United States had recently entered World War I with the intention of making "the world safe for Democracy." Black Memphians recognized the hypocrisy of President Woodrow Wilson's crusade and looked for opportunities to protect themselves at home. Most black southerners continued to live in terror. Many black people thought the NAACP's presence was only reactionary, and it would not prevent the type of violence that befell Ell Persons. The *New York Age* deemed Memphis "the most murderous city on earth." In 1915 there were a reported 122 homicides in the city; New Orleans finished a distant second with 83. Another statistic reveals that, for every 100,000 residents of Memphis, 81.3 were killed; this figure, too, led the nation. The 227 Memphis police officers could not control the outlaw culture that existed in the city.[20] This negligence prompted a response from the black community. The week of Persons's lynching, 1,500 to 2,000 African Americans flooded the bus station in Memphis with the hopes of purchasing a ticket to Chicago. On June 5, a military recruiter came to Memphis with the intention of getting black men to enlist in the military. He had scheduled his trip to Memphis prior to the lynching and expressed his disappointment with the turnout. He expected around 8,000 men between the ages of twenty-one to thirty to enlist; however, only 3,000 showed. The *Commercial Appeal* noted that the few men who did enlist only did so to escape the racist atmosphere of the city. The recruiter believed that "German agents" had sabotaged his trip; however, it was more likely that African Americans were protesting the racial situation in Memphis.[21]

Church could not ignore the reactions of these black Memphians, and for the first time he spoke out against the lynching. Three thousand anxious black men and women packed themselves in Church Auditorium on June 29 to attend the first meeting of the Lincoln League since Persons's death. In the weeks after the burning, no organization publicly condemned the actions of the mob; no leader had come forward to provide advice or guidance, and no one delivered a speech to provide hope and courage to those who desperately needed direction. A newspaper captured the moment: "The pent-up feeling of the patriots and patriarchs, together with a thousand women, found expression in a burst of cheers when Robert R. Church Jr. . . . took the gavel. What the people expected is exactly what they got."[22] Church reassured the crowd, "I would be untrue to you and myself as your elected leader if I should remain silent against shame and crime of lawlessness of any character, and I could not if I would hold my peace against either the lynching or burning of a human being." He encouraged the members, "We must not lose hope, but keep our eyes open and press forward." He concluded his speech by endorsing the work of the NAACP.[23]

The tragedy of 1917 proved that the Lincoln League and the NAACP were necessary for the race's continued progress. Church never contemplated conceding to the threats made by white supremacists or abandoning his political crusade. He instead focused on the state elections of 1918. Church commented to a reporter that he would fight year after year "until the political chains are broken and colored men are treated as citizens." Empowering African Americans politically remained his professional priority. Church, much like generations of African Americans before him, equated the right to vote with freedom. He said, "If the League did nothing more than teach colored men the dignity of the ballot and white men that all colored men cannot be purchased and a great number misled that is enough for the first time." His faction continued their role as the "Regular Republican Party" of Tennessee and began organizing and campaigning.[24]

The Lincoln League remained a strong organization. Its new branches and growing membership raised the concerns of whites throughout the state who did not believe in the league's sustainability. Newspaper writers began to voice their concerns more regularly. They questioned the leadership of Church. They depicted him as a dictator and not a person who truly believed in the democratic process. The *Nashville Banner,* for instance, thought African Americans should take initiative and vote for the candidates they thought fit without Church's influence. An editorial in the *Banner* warned members of the Lincoln League that if African American voters continued to vote based on the "dictation of the League . . . they will invite a solid white opposition."[25] The editorial scolded league members and reminded its leaders that their main goal should be to encourage its members to make individual judgment in voting and not to be herded to the polls like obedient cattle.

Church's political strategies demanded that the members of the organization look to him and other leaders in the league for their political direction. Although the *Banner*'s argument is rooted in logic, it is not a fair assessment of Church or the league. White supremacist organizations had compromised the essence of democracy long before the league's existence. In fact, it was the actions of the Shelby County Republicans that made the Lincoln League a necessary organization. The league was formed as a reaction to the solid white opposition that existed in the South. White Democrats worked diligently to keep African Americans second-class citizens; lily-white Republicans were even more inclined than Democrats to refuse them any form of political representation. Therefore Church had to develop a program that strove toward achieving assimilationist ends through separatist means.[26]

The *New York Age* highlighted the shortcomings of the *Banner*; "the spectacle of a southern daily preaching against race solidarity in politics is a bit unusual not to say incongruous." Church established the Lincoln League to involve African Americans in the democratic process, not to compromise its democratic principles. He told members of the league that he had no intention of assuming a revolutionary role or forming "a color line organization similar to the Ku Klux Klans." He wanted the members of the league to ascribe to the same type of idealism as the Young Turks movement and the Sons of Liberty during America's prerevolutionary days. Church worked to strengthen the organization and make them a closer-knit group. The construction of black institutions such as political organizations, fraternal orders, schools, and colleges could produce "mainstream values . . . in a segregated environment."[27]

Church responded to the limits of the Jim Crow South the best way that he knew. However, his "racial uplift" strategies reveal a disconnect between the leaders and members of organizations such as the Lincoln League. Church told members of the league exactly who they should vote for in local, state, and national elections. He expected no one to deviate from this plan and, according to the evidence, few did. Church's demanding leadership style eventually earned him the nickname of "the roving dictator of the Lincoln Belt."[28]

Although Church embraced a more egalitarian vision of racial uplift, his form of leadership bordered on paternalism. Certain aspects of his uplift ideology were fundamentally contradictory. As historian Kevin Gaines states, "Elite African Americans were replicating even as they contested, the uniquely American racial fictions upon which liberal conceptions of social reality and equality were founded. . . . Although uplift ideology was by no means incompatible with social protest against racism, its orientation toward self-help implicitly faulted African Americans for their lowly status, echoing judgmental dominant characterizations of the Negro problem."[29]

Wilson Moses describes this ideology as a form of "black bourgeois nationalism" that existed from the 1850s through the 1920s. Although members of the black elite viewed themselves as separate from working-class blacks, they too had to deal with the reality that they were also denied access to mainstream institutions based solely on their race. Therefore, leaders such as Church emphasized ideas of "group self-consciousness" and developed programs that attempted "to manipulate the hostile environment in which it was conceived." Church and other "black bourgeoisie nationalist" leaders developed an "alternative structure, a functional tradition created for publicizing black aspirations, giving them political force, and institutionalizing them in forms that might ultimately transform American civilization."[30] Church and other leaders during the Jim Crow era wanted to advance the race; however, there was no clear indication as to how this could be achieved.

Church's programs did provide a real sense of optimism for African Americans in the state, and this further enraged his enemies. Church's friend and protégé George W. Lee discussed tactics used by influential white politicians to have him drafted into the army and fight in World War I. White Republican leaders wanted to eliminate Church as a leader, destroy the Lincoln League, and seize total control of the Republican Party in West Tennessee. Lee stated, "even though he had a wife, a daughter, a sister, and a mother who were all dependent members of his household, he wrote across the top of the questionnaire, 'I claim no exemption.'" Whites viewed Church as a "dangerous radical" and wanted to thwart his authority. Despite his enemies' efforts, the military never called Church for duty. He remained steadfast in his approach and sought to control the Republican Party in the state.[31]

The Lincoln League focused on the state elections of 1918. That year the Republican State Committee sat Church as a full member in the organization. His white rival, John Farley, spoke out against Church's seat: "he did not care for a seat to the committee if Mr. Church had a seat there."[32] J. Will Taylor, state committee chairman, informed Farley that the political leaders of Tennessee agreed that "Mr. Church had the only organization in the state, and that henceforward he was to be considered as the leader of Shelby County and the Tenth district, where he controls more votes than all the lilies combined."[33] Church grew tired of Farley and the antics of "water-through Republicans and suitcase Democrats," and in July 1918 he announced his candidacy for membership on the Republican State Executive Committee. Church represented the Tenth District, comprised of Tipton, Hardeman, Fayette, and Shelby counties. He had successfully mobilized the black vote in West Tennessee during the previous national elections and knew that he could easily defeat any lily-white opposition. The last black person to be elected to this seat was Josiah T. Settle, twenty years prior. His friends, influential black Memphians Thomas Hayes, Bert Roddy, and "Little Joe" Settle, campaigned on Church's behalf. The *Chicago Defender* reported that everyone had a poll tax receipt that dated prior to July 1, 1918, to ensure they could register. The *Defender* stated, "No contest has attracted so much attention in a while, for everybody who knows that Church is one man that they can't steal from and get away with it."[34]

On July 19, Roscoe Conkling Simmons spoke to an estimated five thousand citizens of both races at Church Auditorium. Simmons, regarded as one of the leading orators of his era, declared "the day of political emancipation of the South was at hand for the first time in years." As expected, Church was elected as a member of the Republican State Committee and the State Republican Primary Board. He and the Lincoln League "snapped the political chains of the south." The Democrats and Republicans withdrew their candidates the day before the election, and Church won full membership to the State Executive Committee and the State Republican Primary Board.[35] As the *Defender* reported, "the lily-whites were afraid to go to the mat with him." Church told Simmons that the reason the Republicans withdrew their candidates was because "they did not want my strength to become a matter of public record, and they knew that if they held the Primary they couldn't steal it, and they couldn't get me to withdraw."[36]

The person with whom Church most wanted to share his success, Sallie, could not be with him to celebrate. She suffered from an illness suspected to be cancer, and she was living with her mother in Washington, D.C. He wrote her on their wedding anniversary and congratulated her for "being able to put up with me for seven years." He informed her of his election and sent her a copy of a letter written by Jim Europe, a world-renowned musician, with the hopes of lifting her spirits. Church enclosed some money and assured her the "baby [Roberta] is well and doing fine." Annette served as the primary caretaker for Roberta while Sallie was away. With a heavy heart Church ended the letter like he always did, "Devotedly yours, Robert."[37]

Congratulatory letters from other family members and other prominent leaders flooded his office. Ida B. Wells recognized him for his "splendid victory." She offered, "I know that you will do great things for your people. I am certainly proud of your father's son, my only regret is that he could not have lived to enjoy your victory." Apparently Wells had also fallen on hard times, and she reminded Church of the time his father loaned her $200 to return to Memphis after being stranded in California. In the same letter she asked Church if she could borrow $500. "If I had not given my life, and all I could earn to help this race of ours, I would not need to ask such a favor of any one," said Wells. She added, "Having done so, and the race at large having benefitted by my work, I feel I have the right to ask such a favor of one of my old friends who is amply able to do this for me."[38]

He took his seat in September 1918. The crowd gave him an "ovation that strong men only give to a strong man."[39] Church's victory was an important individual accomplishment, but it meant more for the race. The other members of the committee welcomed Church and congratulated him on his victory. His triumph provided an opportunity to discuss the issues that plagued Tennessee's African American community with the Republican Party's elite politicians.

In addition to Church, the Lincoln League had elected nineteen of the twenty winners of various local elections, including Mayor Frank Monteverde and County Trustee Edward "Boss" Crump. Church wrote to Roscoe Simmons that "the Lincoln League did its duty well, and the members deserve a lot of credit."[40] He also instructed Simmons to publish an article in the *Defender* because "I think it is one of the greatest victories we have ever won." He continued: "get this done in the paper this week and the next time I see you I will buy you a package of peanuts." Robert Abbott, owner of the *Chicago Defender*, had recently hired Simmons as the newspaper's public relations representative at $125 weekly. Simmons could command an audience with his writings and speeches, unlike Church, who was an average orator at best. A newspaper article described Simmons as an amazing genius who was "the ambassador of 12 million people, the wisest champion his Race ever had, and his country's foremost orator."[41] Church consulted with Simmons perhaps more than any other person on political issues. *The Defender* had a national readership, and Simmons often used his articles to promote the achievements of Church and the League.

Church had developed the Lincoln League into a political powerhouse and hoped to carry this momentum into the fall as he worked with the leaders of the league to develop strategies for the state elections. The Lincoln League endorsed Republicans H. B. Lindsay for governor, H. C. Evans for U.S. Senate, and George C. Taylor for state railroad commissioner. A circular generated by the league read, "nothing is more important in the present than breaking our political chain. Second in importance is to stand by with those who give a hand when it takes a man to give the hand. . . . The results will be close and we can win if you do your part."[42] Although nearly one thousand of the league's members in Shelby County voted for the Republican candidates, they still could not overcome the Democrats' control over the rest of the state. Church continued to suffer political defeats at the hands of the Democrats, but he was winning the fight against the lily-whites as more counties in West Tennessee began to align themselves with Church's Republican candidates.

Church succeeded in educating and organizing black voters in West Tennessee, but the party remained divided. The Republican National Committee saw the potential for securing a Republican following in the South based on the work of Church. Perhaps other black Republicans in the region might prove that they could mobilize black voters. Church demonstrated that he could raise funds for the party, as well. Since he financed his own organizations and programs and paid his way to conventions, he became a financial asset for the party. In preparation for the state elections of 1918, the GOP changed its tactics and demanded more reform in the South. It also wanted a united party. In 1918 the Republican Party appointed Will H. Hays as its national chairman because of his effectiveness as a conciliator, and one of his main priorities was unifying the party. Hays contacted Church, informing him that "your name has been suggested to me . . . as one whom we can depend upon in Tennessee." He asked Church to partner with other respected Republican leaders and prepare a document that informed him of the state's most pressing issues. He hoped to benefit from Church's "suggestion and advice at all times." Hays's appointment to the national committee marked the beginning of a long political relationship between him and Church, and helped to increase Church's presence in the national organization.[43]

Church had aligned himself with the most powerful politicians of his era, as well as the era's most successful civil rights organization, the NAACP. For Church to accomplish his goals of mass political mobilization among African Americans, he needed to extend his presence beyond Tennessee. His affiliation with the NAACP likely helped to grow the organization as well as his political machine. Most southern states had stricter voting restrictions than Tennessee. With the presence of lily-white Republicans and the obstacle of disfranchisement, some southern black men became increasingly uninterested in politics, and were more likely to vote without partisan bias. Neither party made sincere appeals to black voters. As Glenda Gilmore suggested, no one could blame black southerners if they held "a perfectly human tinge of malice toward the Republican at the polls."[44] Church's presence within the Republican Party and the NAACP allowed him to merge these separate institutions to appeal to the concerns of the black community. During the World War I era, "southern African Americans began to look toward the NAACP as a way to express political opinions."[45] His affiliation with the NAACP also allowed Church the opportunity to expand his position beyond politics and develop a larger constituency.

Church also had to consider the political effects of the Great Migration. Although the war created opportunities for blacks "to taste industrial freedom" in the North, the exodus ironically "elevated the possibilities for those who stayed behind." White southerners had grown accustomed to a dependent black labor force. They realized the value of black labor in providing the "Negro race the chance to register its first protest against its treatment in the South." The conditions in the South allowed the NAACP the opportunity to "translate ideals into action." Their service in the armed forces allowed African Americans to reassert claims to "full citizenship rights, while exposing how America's racial caste system undermined the nation's most fundamental values." For the first time in its near-decade of existence, the NAACP could truly become a national organization. Church would play a considerable role in their efforts.[46]

Now Church was given the task of helping to establish more charters throughout the South. The newly appointed executive secretary, John R. Shillady, and the NAACP's president, Moorefield Storey, had devised plans for a drive that would increase membership in the organization by fifty thousand members. They called upon Church to assist in the aims of the national organization. Church invited James Weldon Johnson and Shillady to speak at a meeting that would be hosted by the Memphis branch on May 24, 1918. He told Johnson that he could secure at least "two or three thousand" people in attendance. The meeting was billed as "a big Monster Mass Meeting" to be held at Church's Park. It aimed to educate Tennesseans on the objectives of the NAACP.[47] Following the meeting, Church provided the names and addresses of several leading men in Chattanooga and Nashville who were eager to establish branches despite the constant threat of violence that paralyzed the region. Church impressed the national office with his ability to mobilize large crowds on short notice, and much like the Republican Party, the NAACP's leaders in New York knew he could be a financial asset for the national organization.

The NAACP needed a respected black southerner who understood the culture of the South and could convince his peers to establish charters in their cities and towns. Following the meeting in Memphis, Church emerged as a key component in growing the organization and aiding them with their national antilynching campaign.[48]

The NAACP's antilynching campaign was inspired by the efforts of a Republican congressman from St. Louis by the name of Leonidas Dyer. In the aftermath of the Persons lynching and the 1917 East St. Louis riots, Dyer introduced an antilynching bill that promised to "guard citizens of the United States against lynching" based on compliance with the Fourteenth Amendment.[49] This bill served as a motivating force for the NAACP's thirty-year antilynching crusade. That same year the NAACP made an important hire by appointing Walter White to his new position as assistant field secretary. Within two weeks of White's hiring, he traveled to Tennessee to investigate the lynching of Jim McIlherron in Estill Springs, Tennessee. Although it is unlikely that White stayed with the Churches during his investigation, the Church home usually accommodated White during his travels to Memphis and the Delta region. After a visit to the Churches in December 1918, he wrote Anna to thank the family for its hospitality: "I have never enjoyed so thoroughly a visit in all my experience as I did the all too few days spent there and I shall always remember them with the keenest pleasure." Growing tired of his road travels, he jokingly concluded, "I suppose I'll get my resting in Heaven, if I ever get there, although I am afraid the Crackers won't let me."[50]

For his efforts in attempting to establish branches in the region and to pass antilynching legislation, Johnson informed Church that he planned to nominate him to serve as a member of the NAACP Board of Directors. Johnson, a native southerner, felt the South should have some representation on the board. In January 1919, the NAACP announced in its *Bulletin* that Church had become the first exclusively southern member of the organization's board. Church had helped to establish sixty-eight branches in fourteen southern states. He became the representative of 9,841 members in a region that two years prior had virtually no presence. Church had personally grown the membership in the Memphis branch to over 1,000 members.[51] His success in the region established a trustworthy and capable liaison with the national office. Church used his contacts in the region to provide news and information during preliminary investigations, and he used his influence to grow the NAACP in Tennessee and surrounding states.[52]

In the following years, the Church family home often served as a headquarters for lynching investigations in Tennessee, Mississippi, and Arkansas. Church would dispatch informants and reporters to various areas to gather information about lynchings, riots, and other discriminatory practices to share the findings with the national office, preparing White or Johnson for their personal investigations. The NAACP Executive Committee was always suspicious of infiltration and would instruct Church to monitor the behavior of persons affiliated with the organizations, such as branch leaders, attorneys, and investigators. They also did not want the correspondence between Church and the national office to be intercepted and their work sabotaged. Therefore, a select few members communicated in a secret code while they discussed the details of certain lynchings. NAACP press official Herbert Seligmann created the system to gather news from the South. He urged Church to use the following code:[53]

| Code | Equivalent |
| --- | --- |
| Purchased Memphis (or other city) | Man lynched at Memphis (or other city) |
| George purchased Memphis or other city | Woman lynched at Memphis or other city |
| 1500 (or other number) | By mob of 1500 or other number |
| Cash | Charge of rape |
| Mortgage | Charge of attack on woman or other offense against woman |
| Clear | Charged with other offense |
| Sale Memphis (or other city) 100 (or other number of dollars) | Race riot Memphis (or other city) in which 100 (or other number) Negroes injured |
| Credit Memphis (or other city) | Your representative in Memphis (or other city) |
| Wire funds | Recommend immediate investigation |
| Forward shipment Memphis (or other city) | Advise by wire of developments at Memphis (or other city) and send clippings |
| Fred | Ku Klux Klan |
| Price raised Memphis (or other city) | Trouble threatened Memphis (or other city) |
| George Hill | H. J. Seligman |
| Alfred Means | J. R. Shillady |
| Harold Phelps | J. W. Johnson |
| Joseph Wild | Walter White |

Church kept the national organization abreast of lynchings, riots, police brutality, white attitudes in the community, and the names of other southern black leaders who wanted to establish NAACP branches. Outside the offices in New York, Church emerged as one of the organization's most valuable members.

Two separate entities, the Republican Party and the NAACP, coveted Church for his ability to mobilize African Americans in support of their efforts. Both white and black national leaders wanted to use Church's attributes to their advantage. The elections of 1916 and 1918, combined with the Ell Persons tragedy, catapulted Church into the upper echelon of black leaders. The Persons lynching forced Church to reassess his leadership style and recognize that political activism moved beyond participation at the polls.

A political structure already existed within black communities in Memphis and other southern cities. African Americans, regardless of class, had built churches, public and private schools, newspapers, fraternal orders, women's auxiliaries, and political organizations. For Church to be successful he needed to recognize that "these institutions composed a formidable and intermeshed infrastructure of social and political engagement." By tapping into these institutions, Church used the existing community to combat lily-whitism, disfranchisement, lynching, and other issues pertinent to the black community.[54]

By serving on the NAACP Executive Board, Church moved from being an exclusively political leader to a more complete civil rights activist. His progress provided an opportunity for blacks who had become disillusioned with the political process with another avenue to express their political opinions. Black people believed that the NAACP worked for them as "sort of a secret agent among southern African Americans."[55] The NAACP became another tool that Church could use to reach a black electorate that would otherwise not be interested in joining a solely political organization. Yet under the auspices of the NAACP, Church could still push his political agenda. He married the social uplift message of the NAACP with traditional politics to create a strategy that made him one of the most influential black leaders for the next decade.

Figure 1. Studio portrait of Robert R. Church Sr.; his wife, Anna Wright Church; and their two youngest children, Robert Jr. and Annette Church. Courtesy of Special Collections Department, University Libraries, University of Memphis.

Figure 2. Robert Church Jr. and his wife, Sara Johnson Church, at Atlantic City, New Jersey, from the 1910s. Courtesy of Special Collections Department, University Libraries, University of Memphis.

Figure 3. Robert Church Jr. holding his daughter, Roberta Church, from the 1910s. Courtesy of Special Collections Department, University Libraries, University of Memphis.

Figure 4. An assembly of the Lincoln League of Tennessee, founded by Robert Church Jr.
1916. Courtesy of Special Collections Department, University Libraries, University of Memph

Figure 5. Prominent black Republican leaders. *From left to right:* Robert R. Church Jr., Henry Lincoln Johnson, Roscoe Conkling Simmons, Walter L. Cohen, John T. Fisher, and Perry W. Howard standing outside the Solvent Savings Bank and Trust Company, 392 Beale Avenue, Memphis. Photo by Hooks Bros. Studios. Courtesy of Special Collections Department, University Libraries, University of Memphis.

Figure 6. Robert R. Church Jr. sitting at his desk surrounded by framed pictures of influential black and white Republican leaders. Courtesy of Special Collections Department, University Libraries, University of Memphis.

# We Return Fighting

I N THE AFTERMATH OF THE Ell Persons lynching, Church emerged as one the NAACP's most important members due to his wealth as well as the strategic position of Memphis as the only major city near the volatile Mississippi Delta. Church would therefore play a key role in several high-profile cases in Tennessee, Mississippi, and Arkansas. Walter White needed Church and his contacts to help establish the New York–based civil rights organization in the South. This increased Church's profile in the organization and among black leaders during the post–World War I era. Two years after offering his home as the headquarters for the Persons lynching investigation, he would be called upon remotely by White to assist with the Elaine, Arkansas, riots during the year commonly referred to as the "Red Summer."

The little town of Elaine, Arkansas, embodied the racial tensions of the nation in 1919. The rural community located in Phillips County, in the heart of the Arkansas Delta, was a quiet farm community that reflected the characteristics of a typical town in the Jim Crow South. Black sharecroppers and tenant farmers, who worked the cotton plantations, found themselves in a position where they had little power in their negotiations with white planters. In most instances, black farmers had to accept whatever their white employers would offer. As second-class citizens, African Americans had few recourses to combat injustices, which allowed for their employers to further infringe on their civil liberties. Employers dictated nearly every aspect of African American life.[1]

On September 30, approximately 150 to 200 black sharecroppers cramped into the tiny Hoop Spur Church in Phillips County. Frustrated with the mistreatment by their employers, the county's black workers organized to form the Progressive Farmers and Household Union of America (PFHUA). The PFHUA agreed not to pick or sell cotton until its members received fair market value from their landlords. At the time the market value of cotton in Arkansas was forty-five cents a pound, but white planters would only pay black farmers twenty-four cents. Men, women, and children attended the meeting that night to discuss the hiring of a prominent white attorney from Little Rock to represent them. White farmers found out that the black sharecroppers were holding a meeting in the church. Around eleven o'clock, several cars filled with armed white men pulled in front of the church and opened fire, killing a few members. The attendees responded in an act of self-defense and fired shots back at their attackers. In the end a white railroad agent was killed and a deputy wounded.[2]

The horrified white community thought black sharecroppers had launched a full-fledged insurrection with intentions to kill the white landowners in the area. Arkansas Governor Charles Brough requested and received 600 federal troops to quell the suspected attacks from the black community. Following orders, the military began arresting suspected black unionists and admittedly killed black people "for refusing to halt when so ordered or for resisting arrest."[3] White vigilantes also indiscriminately shot and killed an unknown number of black people within a two-hundred-mile radius. Estimates of black fatalities ranged from 200 to 300 during the weeklong riot. In its aftermath, a Phillips County grand jury indicted 122 African Americans and charged 73 with murder. Twelve of those men received death sentences. The military made hundreds of other arrests while they tortured and beat black suspects being held in jail.[4]

The NAACP and Walter White immediately began to investigate the incident. Elaine was located approximately ninety miles southwest of Memphis. Prior to leaving for Elaine, White contacted Church to gain more knowledge from sources he had in the area. Church reached out to some people he knew to prepare White for his visit. When White arrived, he posed as a white reporter for a Chicago newspaper and interviewed the governor, local white officials, and the jailed defendants to construct a story that contradicted the claims made by the mainstream media and the state. His report, along with later ones by Ida B. Wells, gained national attention. The NAACP and the local Citizens' Defense Fund Commission raised approximately $10,000 for the defense of the twelve men sentenced to death.[5]

The NAACP Board of Directors named Colonel G. W. Murphy, a prominent white attorney from Little Rock, the lead lawyer for the case. The NAACP strategically chose Murphy because of his race and influence in the area. They rejected an offer from Thomas J. Price, a black lawyer from Little Rock and a member of the NAACP, to serve as legal representation for the case. Price and another black lawyer from the area, Scipio A. Jones, had conducted their own investigations and were trying to build a case to save the lives of the twelve death-row inmates. Price told Walter White that he and Jones planned to "lay the foundation to carry the cases to the United States Supreme Court if need be."[6] He asked the NAACP to help them raise approximately $10,000 for their efforts.

White and other members of the national branch considered the proposal. However, they knew a black lawyer stood little to no chance of overturning the decision for the twelve men in the racist atmosphere of Phillips County, especially if they were affiliated with the NAACP. Initially, the NAACP diverted any attention away from the organization until they had gathered all the evidence they could to stop the executions. It did not want to prompt a response from the white community and ruin its hard work. Although the NAACP hired Murphy, it did not necessarily trust him. James Weldon Johnson wrote Church to inform him that they had hired Murphy and agreed to "pay him $3000 for his services," but they wanted "action and results." He told Church that the national staff held a meeting and decided to ask him "to undertake the task of keeping a check on Colonel Murphy as best you can." Johnson continued, "We do not wish to write or communicate with Colonel Murphy in any way which would cause him to think that we did not have the fullest confidence in him. Nevertheless, we feel that we ought to be in direct touch with him through one of our directors." Johnson instructed Church to send a confidential letter to discover "what you know and what you can find out about Colonel Murphy's standing as a man in the state and as a lawyer, and as to his attitude toward colored people."[7]

Johnson trusted that Church could find out more about Murphy without jeopardizing the case. He made it clear that he did not want any publicity about the Elaine violence "until we are out of the woods." Johnson assured Church, "If we save these men we will flood the country with publicity on what we have done, but publicity now will not help us and will only hurt them." He then asked Church to inform Thomas Price of the NAACP's strategy and to help secure witnesses for the case. He told Church that the national members of the NAACP "felt that you were exactly the man to diplomatically handle this situation as well as to keep your finger on Colonel Murphy's pulse."[8]

Church then helped to organize the investigation on the local level. With a small network of people, he worked on the case, risking their positions and businesses, homes, families, and lives. They faced a constant threat of danger. One person who fled the scene on the day of the riot wrote Church and the other members of the NAACP to explain his experiences. He urged them, "Please get up at once for my help because if they get me, they will kill me."[9] The mob had found literature with the names of men who supported the organization. Though they lived as far as a hundred miles away, they were being terrorized by local whites and sentenced to prison. Violence paralyzed the area. Just the thought of being associated with the case was enough to get a person killed. Despite the violent atmosphere, Church supported the NAACP and served as middleman during the initial investigations.[10]

Church remained active in the Elaine matter and contributed to the NAACP's legal defense fund. The NAACP was involved in two separate cases. One case, *Ware v. State*, listed the name of Ed Ware and five other men. Another case had Frank Moore and five more defendants. The Arkansas Supreme Court overturned *Ware v. State*, citing that the "jury had failed to state the degree of murder the men were found guilty of committing." The other case reached the U.S. Supreme Court and was overturned in 1923. They argued that "the trial had been dominated by a mob spirit." Church did not contribute much to the actual trials, but he continued to correspond with James Weldon Johnson until the last of the twelve men would eventually be released in 1925.

Church and his correspondence with Johnson and White demonstrate the importance of local leaders in the national struggle. The NAACP could not have been successful without people such as Church, who had knowledge of the area, connections with local leaders, and enough influence to mobilize African Americans into action despite the difficult odds. The NAACP needed Church's expertise in organizing black people to prepare for White's visit, as well as to develop a strategy that would work in the racist atmosphere of Phillips County. Constantly fearful of espionage and infiltrators, the NAACP depended on Church for his advice on whom they should align themselves with to make their efforts a success. After the Red Summer of 1919, Church, who still served as its director of southern branches, would continue to play a role in the investigations of several local cases that the NAACP pursued in the years to come.[11]

As the decade ended, Church found a nation in transition. The "Great War" served as the catalyst for the political, economic, and social movements that defined the post–World War I years and the 1920s. In the war's aftermath, some disillusioned whites dropped out of society and looked to the authors of the "Lost Generation" to articulate their frustrations. Increasing labor tensions prompted the working class to strike for fair wages and basic labor rights, while unrelenting employers sometimes countered these labor demonstrations with bloody force. In 1919, to promote ideas of morality and sobriety, the U.S. Congress passed the Eighteenth Amendment to prohibit the sale and consumption of alcohol, while urbanites and youth rebelled by creating a subculture free of inhibition and sexual mores. The nation was in the midst of transitioning into a modern society.[12]

As mainstream America constructed the image of the "roaring twenties" to describe a decade of protest and individualism, African Americans still faced a common foe, white supremacy. An increase in race riots and lynchings reminded African Americans of their second-class status. However, they also found new ways of combating white supremacy. Black men and women born during the post-Reconstruction era had come of age. They had never been enslaved, and they possessed a sense of entitlement that their parents never had the privilege to develop. They had attended school, worked in professional occupations, and developed a collective consciousness of activism. Black people had grown impatient with government-sanctioned racism and began to demand equal rights. Their activism became evident in the art and literature of the Harlem Renaissance, while Marcus Garvey and the Universal Negro Improvement Association embodied the nationalistic spirit of many black people during the 1920s. Together these ideological strands helped pave the way for the emergence of a "New Negro" mentality. For leaders such as Church to remain relevant, they too had to embrace the more militant spirit of the black masses and harness this new energy.[13]

During the spring of 1919, W. E. B. Du Bois stated, "We stand again to look America squarely in the face and call a spade a spade." In his essay "Returning Soldiers," Du Bois applauded the commitment of black soldiers abroad, but criticized the racism African Americans faced on the home front. Du Bois charged, "But by the God of Heaven, we are cowards and jackasses if now that that war is over, we do not marshal every ounce of our brain and brawn to fight a sterner, longer, more unbending battle against the forces of hell in our own land. . . . We return. We return from fighting. We return fighting." Du Bois's comments about the black freedom struggle proved prophetic; they described the orgy of violence that occurred during those summer months.[14]

A militant white opposition determined to keep blacks in their place countered any perceived gains made by African Americans during the Great War. Black soldiers fought to protect democracy abroad while maintaining hope that their country would realize its own hypocrisy and embody the true ideals of a free nation. As these black veterans returned home, they witnessed a renewed commitment by white southerners to reestablish their dominance. Benjamin Mays, then a young college student, noticed, "In many a local community Negro soldiers were told, 'Take off those uniforms and act like a nigger should.'" Extralegal violence resurged. Mays later became a respected preacher, civil rights activist, president of Morehouse College, and is often cited as the mentor of Dr. Martin Luther King Jr. Tuskegee Institute recorded seventy-six lynchings in 1919 compared to thirty-seven in 1917, which had the lowest reported total since the institute began gathering statistics in 1882. Twenty of the victims that year were black veterans. Even more suffered beatings, many while still in uniform, and were forced to leave their homes. A newspaper article stated, "Negro soldiers returning from the war inflamed their people with stories of race equality in Europe, especially the lack of discrimination in social intercourse." Soldiers came home to defend themselves just as they did abroad. That summer in Chicago, and in Tulsa, Oklahoma, in 1921, black soldiers armed themselves and led the charge in defending their communities from their white neighbors, many of whom paid for their actions with their lives. In 1919, over four hundred blacks and whites were killed in various racial insurrections. The "New Negro" mentality infuriated southern whites, who worked once again to redefine their culture through violent means.[15]

That year, thirty-eight race-related riots erupted across the nation. The working class, comprised of both blacks and whites, organized and staged labor protests to improve their economic conditions in the wake of the

Great War; African Americans witnessed President Wilson negotiate the articles for the League of Nations abroad while vigilante terror loomed over their communities. Blacks and working-class whites in general became more militant in their quest for protection and economic security at home. Yet the federal government launched a malicious campaign of anti-communism and xenophobia to keep protesters from challenging the authority of the government and industrialists. America's attention was diverted from the bloody conflicts of the Red Summer and replaced with the anti-Bolshevik campaign of the "Red Scare." The racial implications behind many of the riots that summer were now masked with "antiradical and nativist hysteria." As scholar Kenneth Janken explains, "whites perceived African Americans' attempts to improve their life circumstances as unpatriotic efforts to bring down the social order." The ever-present threat of lynching and mob violence posed a far greater threat to American society than the perceived dangers of Bolshevism. If Church and other leaders spoke out against these ills, they now risked being labeled as communists or un-American.[16]

That summer African Americans responded to the violent antics of whites with violence of their own. They realized that they could not rely on government intervention; they had to protect their families, homes, and businesses themselves. Ida B. Wells commented, "The Negro cannot understand why it was a brave thing to kill the Germans and not equally brave to kill white Huns in his own country, who take his life, destroy his home, and insult his manhood every step of the way in free America."[17] As the working class protected itself in the streets, Church and the NAACP worked to expose the hypocrisy of America and allow the international community to witness the plight of African Americans, especially in the South.[18]

Church publicly supported the "war for democracy" not only as a symbol of patriotism, but also to force the American government to recognize African Americans' inalienable rights as American citizens. In 1918, black Memphians proved their loyalty to America by contributing $174,823 for Thrift Stamps used to finance the war. That fall Church, Bert Roddy, Thomas Hayes, Thomas O. Fuller, James W. Lane, and other prominent blacks from West Tennessee pledged to double their quota of $75,000 for the United War Work campaign. Despite these displays of loyalty by black Tennesseans, the U.S. government refused to protect its African American citizens at home. Black leaders merely wanted America to practice what it preached. Instead, the violence that ensued throughout the state of Tennessee and beyond made a mockery of their efforts.[19]

"The brutality of white violence and the blatancy of economic and legal coercion shocked black leaders who had rallied support for the war and infuriated many younger Negroes," wrote Lester Lamon.[20] A "New Negro" emerged because of America's betrayal to its own citizens. The black community grew tired and would no longer idly stand by and watch their homes, property, and lives be destroyed by racist whites. Claude McKay in his poem "If We Must Die" articulated the mindset of many African Americans: "Like men we'll face the murderous, cowardly pack, / Pressed to the wall, dying, but fighting back."[21] Black leaders who had previously shunned any form of violent retaliation from the black community now began to consider armed self-defense. W. E. B. Du Bois, in his defense of armed resistance, wrote in *The Crisis*: "For three centuries we have suffered and cowered. No race ever gave Passive Resistance and Submission to Evil longer, more piteous trial. Today we raise the terrible weapon of Self-Defense. When the murder comes he shall no longer strike us in the back. When the armed lynchers gather, we too must gather armed. When the mob moves, we propose to meet it with bricks and clubs and guns."[22] Church told NAACP officials in 1919 that "antagonism between the races" was growing in West Tennessee, and he warned the Memphis mayor, Frank Monteverde, that although black Memphians would not instigate any exchanges with the white community they would be prepared to "defend themselves" if attacked.[23]

Southern blacks and whites had opposing views on how race would be defined in the postwar South. Both sides became more radical in their approach. Although Church was well connected with powerful whites, his loyalty remained with the black community. African Americans looked to Church to use his influence with the NAACP and the Republican Party to express their frustrations and distrust for the federal government. The NAACP looked to Church to assist with the ongoing investigations throughout the Delta region and bring justice to the black victims of the Red Summer. The Republican Party looked to Church to convince the black community to trust in the same government that had abandoned them in their time of need. The summer of 1919 exposed the contradictions of the "war for democracy," and now Church had to convince a disillusioned African American voting base to once again believe in the democratic process as he began developing political strategies for the upcoming 1920 national elections.[24]

The Republican Party could no longer take African Americans for granted, and Church needed to highlight the issues in the black community. As blacks fled the South they also found new political opportunities in the North. As a member of the NAACP Board of Directors, Church constantly corresponded with other executive members, and he became directly familiar with countless cases of racial injustice. Because of his position, he was continuously updated on issues pertaining to African Americans regarding education, violence, police brutality, and discrimination. He also learned more about the increasing African American discontent with both political parties. Although Church still believed politics was the most pragmatic approach to bring about equality in America, he certainly was not naive about the problems that existed within his party. In preparation for the 1920 elections, Church challenged the leadership of the GOP to keep its promises or lose the support of African Americans forever. Church capitalized on the information he received as the director of the NAACP's southern branches, attempting to merge the activism of the NAACP with the platform of the Republican Party.[25]

During its national convention in Atlanta, the NAACP challenged both political parties to address the "Negro Question." As both Republicans and Democrats prepared for their respective national conventions, the NAACP called upon them to embrace the principles of justice and democracy for all American citizens. Specifically, the NAACP asked the parties to support African Americans' right to vote, the federal suppression of lynching, national aid for education, and legislation that prohibited segregation in their political platforms. Church emphasized these points in his correspondence with Republican National Chairman Will Hays just months prior to the NAACP meeting. Together Church and Hays worked on a platform that addressed the concerns of African Americans. Church made Hays aware that African Americans were losing faith in the Republican Party, continuously warning him that, if the GOP did not start to follow through on its political platforms, then the black community would begin to exercise other political options.[26]

Younger African American voters who did not embrace the idealized image of Lincoln's party had begun to distance themselves from the GOP and consider other alternatives, such as the Socialist Party. In August 1919, Church commented that the "I.W.W.'s are awake and the Socialists are not asleep," warning of the possible exodus of black voters from the Republican Party.[27] The summer of 1919 demonstrated that the conditions of black people had not improved, and even those who left the South to seek refuge and jobs in the North still experienced discrimination. More than looking for civil rights, black voters heading into the 1920 election wanted help from anyone who was willing to go into their communities and provide protection from ruthless white southerners who were desperate to uphold white supremacy. More African Americans felt they could no longer remain loyal to the Republicans without considering alternative factions. Church warned Hays, "It is claimed the black man cannot expect social and political equality from either one of the old parties, and it is therefore pointed out that the Negro must look to some other source for his political salvation."[28] Church had always been as critical of the party as he was supportive. He recognized that his position extended beyond endorsing Republican leadership, and that the GOP must also be used as a vehicle to improve the status of black people. To Hays he explained, "There is no question confronting the Republican leaders half as important as the question affecting the relationship of the Republican Party to its colored adherents." Black voters, he insisted, were "still the most valuable asset that the party can claim." He charged that present Republicans lacked the perceived integrity of its predecessors and "have either forgotten or are forgetting the loyalty of the colored Republicans."[29]

In 1919, Church warned Hays that Republicans needed to meet face-to-face with black voters, especially the younger generation, to address the "sting of disregard that marks leading Republicans everywhere."[30] In order to repair the damage Republicans caused, Church thought the national organization should speak to the issues plaguing the black community in the leading "colored" and Republican newspapers throughout the country every week. He suggested that Hays hire Roscoe Conkling Simmons to give three to four speeches a week, making sure that he be introduced as a Republican. Finally, Church suggested that Hays be the first Republican leader to speak out against disfranchisement and lynching at his next public meeting. Throughout their correspondence that summer, Church assured Hays that he could still mobilize the black vote for the Republican Party, but he also promised him that they would hold him and the entire party accountable if they won the presidential election.[31]

Church continued to correspond regularly with Hays heading into the fall. Church stressed the importance of having a "colored man" present at all sessions during the upcoming national convention. He urged Hays to follow his advice if he wanted to maintain African American support. The situation of black America prompted Church to "ring the warning bell," outlining the course of action that should be taken to maintain black support.[32] Simultaneously, Republicans also needed to focus on strengthening their presence in the South. White southerners did not disfranchise black people based solely on race; they also disfranchised African Americans because they voted Republican. As indicated by Church's relationship with Boss Crump, if black people supported the Democratic ticket, white southerners would be more likely to repeal laws that stripped African Americans of their political voice. Politics and race placed African Americans in a powerless position in the South, and Republicans needed to be mindful of the sacrifices blacks made in support of their party. Church's mission exceeded securing basic voting rights. Instead he attempted to use the Republican Party to improve the social and economic status of southern blacks. He envisioned that he could eventually transform the Republican Party from a political faction to an instrument used to obtain civil rights.[33]

Church relied on a small network of dedicated leaders in the South to aid his political mission. He recommended to Hays other respected black Republicans who could mobilize black voters. Church welcomed 1920 by working with Hays to develop the Committee on Policies and Platform. Hays wanted the committee to represent "all groups in interest and party thought."[34] He emphasized that Church should suggest "the most representative men and women who are outstanding figures in the different lines of activity, so as to bring the character and ability to the committee which will be of real value."[35] Church considered Hays's request and recommended his friends Roscoe Conkling Simmons, James Weldon Johnson, Boston lawyer William H. Lewis, and Georgia Republican Henry Lincoln Johnson for the committee. All of these men had strong followings and could effectively usher voters to the polls in November. Church also advised Hays to ignore the requests made by the successors of Booker T. Washington in the Tuskegee machine, Emmett Scott and Robert R. Moton. Both leaders had been affiliated with Wilson's administration, and Scott would eventually be appointed special advisor of black affairs. Despite their status, Church did not believe they could be trusted, and black people would not rally behind individuals who held prominent positions in Woodrow Wilson's racist administration.[36]

Church continued to advise Hays that black voters had grown impatient with the GOP and that mere political rhetoric would no longer secure their votes. Republicans needed to take action and produce. Church made high-ranking members of the Republican Party aware of the black community's grievances. Although he could not force the presidential aspirants to recognize these issues on their individual platforms, he made them aware of the consequences if they ignored blacks' concerns. Black people were willing to align themselves with any person, party, or organization that could bring them refuge. Church helped place the concerns of his community into the national political discourse. If he exposed racial injustices, no political candidate could justifiably act as if these problems did not exist. By educating the nation of the black plight, Church put white politicians in a position where they could either help the black community or be exposed as insensitive racists. Church spread the word publicly through newspapers and privately in his correspondence. Church surely knew that not everyone would fall in line and adhere to these demands. However, this blatant disregard of the country's black citizens, combined with the increasing political sophistication of African Americans, served as the backdrop to the era's struggle for black freedom.[37]

Hays continued to court both black and white southerners on behalf of the Republican Party, but more black voters still needed an arena where they could speak openly and freely with their leader. Church used the Lincoln League to develop a strong following. Republicans also attempted to court white southerners, but Church knew that black voters had the potential of impacting state and national elections. He and Roscoe Conkling Simmons attempted to increase the league's presence beyond Tennessee and develop it into a national organization. As historian Elizabeth Gritter stated, "A cross section of black leadership traveled to the two-day meeting in the summer of 1919 at the famed Iroquois Club on Canal Street in New Orleans," where labor leaders sat "side by side with black professionals," to launch the Lincoln League of America.[38] Black leaders in other states contacted Church to establish branches in their hometowns. For instance, Church traveled to Denver, Colorado, to meet with local leaders to set up a branch that would soon boast over one thousand members. Ostracized by local lily-white factions and much of the national GOP, the Lincoln League grew from an alternative local organization into essentially the Republican National Committee for African Americans during the 1920 election season.[39]

Church's organization also benefited from a new group of voters in 1920. Although Church would never be mistaken for a women's rights activist, he learned from his early run-ins with his half-sister Mary and advocated the passage of the Nineteenth Amendment. Tennessee served as the deciding thirty-sixth state to ratify the amendment. As historian Paula Giddings noted, "Church, cognizant of the potential of the female franchise, encouraged the participation of women in the Lincoln League."[40] His friend Ida B. Wells had ended her exile from Memphis, returning to the Bluff City that year to discuss the role of black women in the upcoming election. Meanwhile, Mary crusaded for the passage of what came to be known as the Susan B. Anthony Amendment. She made Church's previous stance on women's suffrage seem foolish, forcing him to recognize his own hypocrisy. He had matured as a leader, and he recognized that black women had a different story that could not be championed solely by men. As Terrell eloquently stated, her story "is a story of a colored woman living in a white world. It cannot possibly be like a story written by a white woman. A white woman has only one handicap to overcome—that of sex. I have two—both sex and race. I belong to the only group in this country which has two such huge obstacles to surmount. Colored men have only one—that of race."[41] The women in the Lincoln League were no longer relegated to positions as teachers and organizers. They now actively participated in all phases of the organization. As Church prepared for the league's convention, he listed several women as delegates, including Ida B. Wells. The Church women—Anna, Annette, and Sallie—had all registered to vote and followed the political contests with keen interest and observation.[42] The Lincoln League now had national appeal and emerged as a more representative organization for all African Americans. Church carried this momentum into the election season.[43]

Church, Roscoe Conkling Simmons, and Henry Lincoln Johnson grew the Lincoln League into a national movement. It became Church's chief instrument for restoring the black franchise and fighting Jim Crow. The scope of the organization, the membership of some of the country's most influential black leaders, and Church's media connections helped to excite a disillusioned voting constituency. The newly formed Lincoln League of America went on the road. It held its first national convention in New Orleans on June 17, 1918. In anticipation of the Lincoln League's arrival, the New Orleans Item proclaimed, "Negroes from Lincoln League to Assist Race: Appeal for Ballot, Curbs on Lynching, Federal Aid for Education."[44]

The article announced the league's officers. Church rarely sought public approval or personal recognition, and true to his personality he declined to serve as the league's president. Yet Church always viewed the league as his very own political machine, and regardless of any official positions within the organization, its members considered Church the "boss."

In preparation for the New Orleans meeting, Roscoe Conkling Simmons served as president, Henry Lincoln Johnson as secretary, and Walter L. Cohen as treasurer. Church served as chairman of the Executive Committee and director. Henry Lincoln Johnson; Perry Howard of Jackson, Mississippi; and W. H. Lewis of Boston composed the legal department. At the convention, delegates from each state elected a vice president who would lead the league's efforts in their state. As a tribute, members of the Lincoln League paid homage to Louisiana's eighty-two-year-old Pinckney Benton Stewart Pinchback, the first African American to become governor during Reconstruction, by naming him honorary president of the convention.[45]

During the meeting, leaders of the Lincoln League first attempted to demonstrate their patriotism by calling for Americans to stand against all foes, foreign and domestic, in the wake of the "Great War." They voiced their concerns for the treatment of returning African American soldiers and pleaded with the government to honor them in the same manner as their white counterparts. They proposed resolutions to address protection at the polls for "all Americans," including black men and women. Members agreed, "The American negro has no desire to control the government of states even where he is most populous. . . . But the negro does ask for a part in the government he is taxed to maintain."[46] Other topics included improving literacy among African Americans, calling for blacks to remain in the South, and urging white southerners to provide equal pay and opportunities for African Americans so that they would not seek these opportunities elsewhere. The Lincoln League's platform also denounced lynching and pleaded for more African Americans throughout the nation to join them in their efforts. The central office would remain in Memphis, where Church could oversee and maintain his daily duties. In New Orleans, Church and his team announced to the nation that the Lincoln League would be a force to be reckoned with during the elections.[47]

The Lincoln League's platform looked more like the goals of a civil rights organization than a strictly political organization. The speakers touched on every major issue concerning the black community at that time.

Although the Lincoln League did not possess the same prestige as the NAACP, its influence should not be overlooked. Much like the NAACP, the Lincoln League was comprised of the leading black politicians, members of the black elite, professionals, and other influential people. However, the Lincoln League was founded, organized, and run exclusively by African Americans, and it still garnered the attention of the nation's political elite. African Americans throughout the nation could take pride in this display of black solidarity and influence. As one newspaper commented, "It is the Race's own organization."[48]

The Lincoln League provided an opportunity for black leaders to meet directly with the masses. With branches in over thirty states, Church and other leaders could develop platforms that would address the universal concerns of the black community. The vice presidents had the responsibility of articulating the specific issues that black people faced in each of their states. Simmons and other members of the media affiliated with the Lincoln League publicized these problems to the nation. Church also brought these concerns to the international stage. He believed that exposing the South's racist indiscretions to larger urban areas, the nation, and ultimately the world would bring shame to the country and perhaps lead to changes. The very existence of the Lincoln League proves that blacks accepted racism as a fundamental flaw in American democracy, but found ways to still participate in the political process.[49]

The Lincoln League captivated black America. The constant flow of applications swamped the league's headquarters. Church had originally scheduled the national convention to take place in Chicago in September, but the overwhelming response forced the postponement of the convention until the following February. Other local political organizations began to change their name to align themselves with the Lincoln League. After careful consideration, Church decided to have the convention February 11–13, 1920, around Lincoln's birthday, as "a fitting celebration to the memory of the great emancipator." As one reporter stated, "All Chicago is on tiptoe for this, the most important Race convention since the Civil war."[50]

In the weeks heading into the meeting Church released the convention platform. Speakers would address the following subjects:

1. Political parties and Colored Americans
2. The government and the colored American soldier.

3. Do we favor cutting down the representation of the disfranchising states: If so, when? If not, why not?

4. The American Federation of Labor and the colored worker.

5. Can the colored railroad worker hold what he has when the railroads are returned to private ownership? If not then what about that fact?

6. How can we best get the news to the American people that the Jim Crow car is eating away the heart of the American nation?

7. Is lynching to be standard of law and order in the United States? If not, who will stop it; how and when?

The leaders of the league attempted to address the issues that resonated most with the majority of African Americans. This convention was an opportunity not only to inspire and rally the support of black voters, but also to put white Republicans on notice. Although much of black America was still recovering from the brutality of the Red Summer, the Lincoln League proved that black people still wanted to display their patriotism, as well as loyalty to a party that had historically turned their backs on them.[51]

Church invited Will Hays to speak at the convention. He wanted the party's spokesman to meet face-to-face with African Americans to ensure black voters that the GOP had not forgotten the true meaning of democracy, and that its leaders would advocate on behalf of the race. This gesture empowered black voters because now they had a person who spoke directly to them, who made promises to improve race relations in America. Church put the GOP's high-ranking officials in a position where they could either address the race problem in America or risk African Americans leaving the party altogether.[52]

On February 11, 1920, black delegates from across the nation packed the South Park Methodist Episcopal Church in Chicago. The interior was decorated with American flags, and an oil painting of Abraham Lincoln overlooked the proceedings. The men wore dark suits while the women were draped in their best dresses and elaborate hats. Over four hundred delegates, representing every state of the union, emphatically answered the roll call. Perry Howard of Mississippi called the convention to order, and the great orator Roscoe Conkling Simmons delivered a "never-to-be-forgotten key-note address."[53] In his resounding voice he described black people as the saviors of American liberty and quoted Lincoln: "They will probably in some trying time to come keep the jewel of liberty in the family of freedom."[54] Simmons gave an inspirational address that resonated with those present at this historic gathering. From there he introduced Republican Chairman Will Hays, one of the few white politicians present at the event. Hays recognized the magnitude of the gathering and reaffirmed that the political future of the Republican Party depended on the support of African Americans. He told the cheering crowd, "Lynching is a crime against judgment and justice, reason and righteousness, an assault on our most sacred institution and is an affront to the accumulated wisdom of past ages. It is a condemnation of Christianity and merits the exoneration of every high minded citizen." His speech was warmly received.[55]

Church and a future U.S. congressman, Oscar De Priest from Illinois, escorted a successful black businessman from Arkansas, Scott Bond, to the platform, where Church and De Priest offered their comments on the status of the race. Every speaker who took to the podium rallied the members to "make America safe for Americans—safe against disfranchisement, against prejudicial labor organizations, against Jim Crow cars, against mob violence and lynching."[56] Members called attention to the Constitution and encouraged its members to see that its provisions were strictly enforced. Several prominent women were in attendance, including Ida B. Wells, who also addressed the convention. The *Chicago Defender* deemed the meeting a "Decided Success" and said of Church that "the race has no finer, none more devoted, no wiser character."[57]

Church had proved that black voters were not "dumb driven cattle" that blindly followed the party's white leaders. The Lincoln League had emerged as a full-fledged race organization. It exceeded its perceived mission of empowering black people through the ballot, becoming an avenue for all African Americans, regardless of class, to voice their concerns to the nation's leading black figures. As the *Chicago Defender* stated, "Our word is no longer to the lilies or the 'big leaders' of the party. That day when we looked to them is gone, forever gone." The article continued, "Our word, and the word of the Race, North and South, is sent not to white men but to The Lincoln League of America."[58]

Even though Hays had delivered a speech at the convention and attempted to endear himself to black voters, he faced criticism from the black media for remaining silent on several causes, including the efforts of lily-whites to drive African Americans out of the party. Lily-whites argued that, if black people were removed from the party, Republicans could increase their membership in the South. Republicans controlled the

Sixty-Sixth Congress and had not passed any substantial legislation that would protect African Americans in the South, most notably the Leonidas C. Dyer antilynching bill.[59]

Many of the Republican presidential candidates neither addressed the grievances of the black community nor pursued the white southern vote. Warren G. Harding emerged as the most dedicated presidential aspirant to court the southerners. He also became the first Republican candidate to campaign in the South in person when he visited Texas. However, he remained mute on the black community's demands heading into the Republican National Convention.[60]

Black Republicans competed for recognition against the lily-white faction for seats at the national convention in Chicago. Church had earned the attention of the GOP's leading national figures, but the fight continued on the local level. In February, Church and four hundred black voters gathered at the Shelby County Republican Convention Hall where thirty white Republicans met them. Church wanted to demonstrate that the Lincoln League represented the regular Republican ticket and should have been recognized accordingly. In response, the white faction hurriedly ran to lock the doors and called the police. After the police arrived, "the Negroes scattered up and down the halls" until Josiah Settle rallied his delegates and announced that they would hold their own convention in the cramped, "tunnel-like hall of the courthouse basement." Church capitalized on the moment and apparently "climbed upon a box at the entrance to the Convention Hall, and elected his own delegates to the Tennessee State Republican Convention."[61] From there his group proceeded to appoint committees and resolutions. According to an interview with Church's "lieutenant" and political successor, George W. Lee, he proclaimed "that if they broke faith with Bob Church and the hopes of the race, the black soldiers who slept in Argonne Forest and the Vosges Mountains would certainly rise up and haunt them."[62] At the impromptu convention, Church's faction selected delegates to do battle with the lily-whites at the state convention.[63]

Church chartered a "Pullman" for his delegation, which would both navigate around the Jim Crow laws on the train and avoid any acts of sabotage that would prevent them from attending the meeting in Chattanooga. Church wanted "colored republicans [to] be more than just members of the Party organization." He demanded that they be recognized as leaders. In April, prior to the official meeting, Church and other members of the

State Executive Committee met at the Patten Hotel in downtown Chattanooga. He pleaded with the committee that the delegates selected at the Shelby County Courthouse be seated at the state convention. After listening to Church's appeals, an unsympathetic Republican State Committee denied Church's request to have black Memphians seated as the regular Republicans from the city, proving again that Republicans would accept black patronage, but not their leadership. In response Church threatened to have the Lincoln League vote for the Democrats in the local and state elections if he and his delegates were not seated. The committee did not budge. Church, along with two hundred other dejected African American delegates from Tennessee, planned a walkout if the committee seated the rival factions.[64]

The next day Church led the black delegates into a tension-filled convention room. As they took their seats, no one knew what to expect from the rival factions. The state committee, as expected, seated the two white factions from Memphis and excluded Church's delegation from any representation. Instead of following through with the proposed walkout, an outraged Church used his political influence. Church sent Will Hays a telegram explaining the committee's segregationist stance, and Hays responded by reprimanding the state leaders and telling them to comply with Church's demands. The following day the state committee reversed its decision in a vote of 333 to 224, seating the African American delegates and allowing them to represent one-third of the votes entitled to Shelby County. Church won the temporary victory, but a larger battle lay ahead at the national convention.[65]

His sister Annette wrote that the family was elated with his victory over the lily-whites, and that she prayed for him to win not because "you were my brother and because you were a colored man but because you were unquestionably right." Annette had eagerly followed the political contests and "read with interest each decision." She also asked him to express her congratulations to Walter Cohen and Henry Lincoln Johnson, as well as her apologies to Perry Howard and several other African Americans who lost their seats. She ended her letter by telling Church that their mother was extremely proud of him for winning, but more importantly for how he conducted himself during the heated exchanges. Although this was the first election in which she could vote, her letter expressed the wisdom of someone who may have been as politically savvy as her brother. Politics had become the new family business.[66]

A seat at the state convention did not guarantee Church's position at the national meeting. Church entered battle with his lily-white rival attorney John W. Farley. Farley argued that Church and other black Republicans hurt the party: "the mass of Negroes by nature cared nothing about voting and preferred to let Anglo-Saxons run the government; only the mulattoes such as Robert R. Church, who had some of the white man's invigorating blood, sought to participate in politics." Farley then invoked the segregationist image of Lincoln to counter his image as the "great emancipator" and quoted him by stating "I will say, then that I am not, nor ever have been, in favor of bringing about in any way the social or political equality of the white and black races."[67]

The National Committee ignored Farley's plea and placed Church as a temporary delegate. However, Mrs. Eddie M. McCall Priest and four other women delegates led the white Memphians' efforts to appeal the Credentials Committee's ruling. She argued that Church had been involved in illegal activities in the city. She claimed Church ran a gambling establishment and owned the largest black-owned dive in the county. Mrs. Priest threatened that, if Church remained seated, then she and other white Memphians would abandon the party altogether. Although the allegations were untrue, Church did not want to engage in a long public battle with Mrs. Priest. He was not as concerned about besmirching his public persona as he was about the consequences of insulting a white woman in the racist atmosphere of West Tennessee. This case stood as another example of how the culture of white supremacy crippled black manhood, preventing Church from reacting to her allegations. Church fully understood the consequences of confronting the women delegates. As he told his friend James Weldon Johnson, he was "too wise" to engage in a fight with Mrs. Priest or the other women, but he wished he could "burn the two men up, who where hiding behind their skirts."[68]

The Credentials Committee voted to have him unseated by a vote of twenty-three to eighteen, and Church did not challenge the decision. Church did, however, seek vindication at the convention after the chairman called on him to deliver the minority report. A composed Church deliberately addressed the convention: "Mr. Chairman, I have a minority report in my hand and I know that I am entitled to a seat in the convention as a delegate from the tenth Congressional District of Tennessee, but I am not going to be the one man to bring in a minority report before this convention, So I have decided to withdraw it and I am going to carry my fight back to Memphis, Tennessee, and settle it there."[69] Church and his delegates then exited the committee. An electrified crowd received Church's short speech with cheers. Reminiscing, George Washington Lee called Church "a trained diplomat who was wise enough to sacrifice the glory of the moment for the commanding place in the future."[70]

Church further endeared himself to the most powerful members of the Republican Party. Will Hays appointed Church as director of the Republican Negro Campaign and provided him with an office in New York. Charles Cottrill, Henry Lincoln Johnson, T. Coleman Dupont, and Jack Henley assisted Church in this new endeavor as they prepared for the presidential elections.[71]

Warren Harding emerged as the Republican candidate for president. Hays advised Harding to make a "strong statement in favor of justice for Negroes in his acceptance speech."[72] As Hays worked with Harding to develop a speech, he corresponded with Church and made him aware that he "really want[ed] to make a great deal out of this speech to colored voters," and he needed to give it some serious thought.[73] On July 22, Harding stated, "the Federal government should stamp out lynching and remove that stain from the fair name of America." Harding like most candidates denounced the practice of extralegal violence. However, he moved beyond the platform of the party and said that he believed that "Negro citizens of America should be guaranteed the enjoyment of all their rights, that they have earned their full measure of citizenship bestowed, that their sacrifices in blood on the battlefields of the republic have entitled them to all of freedom and opportunity, all of sympathy and aid that the American spirit of fairness and justice demands." Some African Americans believed they heard echoes of Lincoln in his speech, while more radical blacks such as A. Philip Randolph believed it was another Republican ploy to capture black support.[74]

Regardless, Church assured Hays that the Lincoln League would secure the black vote for Harding. Church wanted Harding to be aware that the Lincoln League was represented in every region of the country and was "prepared to go on with the work, thus saving you and Mr. Harding the time and thought necessary to perfect an organization from the ground up." Church and James C. Napier campaigned on his behalf throughout the state. Napier, the leading black public figure in Nashville, convinced Hays that he could mobilize the black population in his section of the state, and Church was the black political boss from West Tennessee. Hays and Harding agreed that Tennessee was the one southern state that the GOP could win if they rejected lily-whitism. In addition to the GOP attempting to court the southern vote, this campaign served also as the first major effort to register black women to vote. Church's sister Mary directed the eastern division of the Colored Women's Bureau on behalf of Harding.[75]

Throughout the campaign, Harding and Hays remained in contact with several black leaders including Church, James Weldon Johnson, William Monroe Trotter, Henry Lincoln Johnson, and Perry Howard. Although each urged Harding to take a strong stance on black issues, he tried to appease white segregationists. He thought black people should be protected by the law and given equal rights. However, Harding admitted that he did not believe "white people and black people should be forced to associate together."[76] He was careful not to upset white segregationists with his comments, given the widespread white anxiety that he would be too close of an ally to black people. In his campaign literature, Democratic candidate James Cox responded to Harding's relationships with black leaders by warning northern and southern whites of a "negro" takeover.[77]

Harding did not waver in his alliances with black politicians. Church continued to solicit support for his campaign. The national headquarters sent Church to Maryland and Kentucky to campaign on the party's behalf. Church and members of the Lincoln League directed voter-registration drives, encouraged blacks to pay their poll taxes, and urged people to turn out at the polls in November. As he did four years prior, Church provided a list of candidates he wanted his followers to support in the state and national elections, headlined by Harding for president and Alfred Taylor for governor of Tennessee. Tennessee still held a unique position as compared to other southern states, because blacks could vote in larger numbers. Therefore they represented a real threat in both political contests. The *Nashville Globe* ran the headline "The World Is Watching the Action of the Colored Voters of Tennessee."[78] In the weeks heading into the election, Church called a meeting at Church's Park and Auditorium on Beale Street. An estimated 15,000 people packed the auditorium as they listened to Roscoe Simmons deliver a passionate keynote address. According to Roberta and Annette Church, so many people arrived at the gathering that Simmons had to make an additional speech on the steps of the auditorium for those who could not get inside.[79]

Heading into the final days of the campaign, Hays wrote Church to thank him for his service: "Before we break up housekeeping, I just want you to get this word of appreciation to you. It has been a great fight. We are going to win, and the winning is no accident. I just wanted you to know that the Committee appreciate the efforts put forth by you in the coming victory."[80] On November 6, 1920, 170,000 black Republicans turned out to vote at the polls throughout the state. Although Church still had to adhere to the local machine politics of Boss Crump, he and his own political machine carried Alf Taylor to victory, electing the state's second Republican governor by a margin of over 25,000 votes. He also endorsed J. Will Taylor, who was elected to Congress. Tennessee was the only southern state that Harding carried. To demonstrate the attention Church gained with these victories, the *Western World Reporter* celebrated Church under the headline "Who Swung Old Tennessee Back Into the Columns of the G.O.P.—How the Trick Was Turned," and the *Wilmington Advocate* stated, "To no one man is there so much credit due for the result in Tennessee as to Robert Church."[81]

Church did not single-handedly deliver the vote to Harding, who received 60 percent of the popular vote and won in a landslide. However, through his efforts, he helped to further empower African Americans politically. Beyond mobilizing the black community to the polls, he helped to create a more sophisticated political awareness among African Americans. The Lincoln League provided an institution where black people could communicate directly with the nation's leading Republicans and campaign for full inclusion into American society. Ironically, the efforts of lily-whites to exclude black people from political participation also created an opportunity for Church's organization to thrive. During the height of Jim Crow, individuals such as Church identified with what historian Darlene Clark Hine describes as "the Achilles heel of white Supremacy." "Segregation provided blacks the chance, indeed, the imperative, to develop a range of distinct institutions that they controlled."[82] While Hine describes the creation of parallel professional institutions for black nurses, doctors, and lawyers to maintain themselves, Church essentially created a parallel political institution where African Americans could privately "buttress battered dignity, nurture positive self-images, sharpen skills, and demonstrate expertise"[83] in a political setting. This safe haven for black politics helped to create a form of collective activism that could bring incremental change. The Lincoln League helped to move African Americans from feeling politically estranged to developing a sense of entitlement in America.

Black voters demonstrated in the 1920 elections that they possessed political agency, and as they became more politically savvy their support could no longer be taken for granted. Church placed the concerns of African Americans into the national political discourse. His organization allowed black people, who otherwise might not have known how to express these concerns in a formal political setting, to identify with a larger national movement. Church and other leaders during the 1920s worked to develop a collective political identity that would provide the support necessary for the activist struggles that would come in the following decades. Church taught African Americans that the success of participating in politics could not be measured by victories alone. Bringing the issues to the forefront of American political debate also had value, nurturing the next generation of activists.[84]

After Harding's inauguration, Will Hays contacted the president to inform him of Church's work. He stated, "Without in any way discounting the splendid work done by a great many colored men, the fact is that for many months before election the one outstanding man among all the colored people, in the quality of unselfish and efficient work done, was Mr. Robert R. Church." In the letter he explained that Church was "very wealthy" and "goes about largely at his own expense on our political errands, never taking any salary, and he is a very exceptional individual."[85] Harding rewarded Church by making him the patronage dispenser for African Americans who coveted federal positions. Church had ascended through the ranks of the GOP. He approved many of the federal positions awarded to African Americans during the Harding administration. Although this appeared to be a rewarding experience, it also proved to be taxing, since many patronage seekers looked for Church's seal of approval. For the next year Church would listen to various pleas made for federal positions by African Americans throughout the country. Church had arrived as a national leader, as he looked to use his influence in the Republican Party to hire people who could advance the issues of black community. With the Republicans back in the White House, the future looked promising for black America.[86]

# 5

# Man of Destiny

AFTER BEING ON THE ROAD for the better part of a year establishing himself as a national political powerhouse, Robert Church returned to the familiar sounds of Beale Street blaring out the blues on his way to the office. As he drove his Type 61 Cadillac down Beale, he witnessed the entire spectrum of the black community.[1] The offices of the black elite shared the same street with the city's underworld. Church's protégé, George W. Lee, described Beale Street as "A main street of Negro America where its pulse beat highest, where richly red, dark brown women, hang-jawed country rubes mixed with spruce urban Negroes in an atmosphere pungent with barbecued pig, alive with the music of those who sit around in the cafes trying to ease their souls with readymade song."[2] Beale Street was the Harlem of the South. These were the people and the city that Church fought for. In return, black Memphians embraced him. Other members of the black elite failed to achieve this feat. Black Memphians proudly followed Church in the national news headlines and envisioned him as one of their own. During the 1920s the only other black Memphian who could rival Church's recognition as a hometown hero was the "Father of the Blues," W. C. Handy. Although in separate worlds, these two men created an image of the Bluff City as a progressive black metropolis in the Mid-South. They made the nation aware of Memphis and all it had to offer.[3]

Professionally Church had reached a new high, but he suffered privately. His wife had been sick during the entire Harding campaign. In January 1922, Sallie, Annette, and Roberta moved to Washington, D.C., to stay at the apartments Church owned on Q Street, where her mother cared for Sallie. An emotional Church wrote Sallie that month to inform her that her illness would require surgery. He tried to ease any fears by reassuring her of the improvements in medicine, and he comforted her by telling her she should only be in the hospital for a couple of weeks. Church urged her to have the surgery as soon as possible. He offered her the option of going to any hospital she preferred, whether it was the Mayo Clinic, St. Luke's in Chicago, or Johns Hopkins in Baltimore.[4] That spring Sallie had the operation at Johns Hopkins but never fully recovered. Church had been with her during those months and "never left her bedside." The *Chicago Defender* claimed he "deserted business and politics" to be with his wife during her time of need. Sadly, Sallie passed away on July 3. "Mrs. Church Dies in Washington, Capital Mourns," proclaimed the *Chicago Defender*, remembering Sallie as "one of the most beautiful girls Washington could ever boast." Church, grief-stricken, had lost the woman he had known since "he was a boy in knee breeches and she just a little girl holding her mother's hand."[5] It is hard to measure how he coped with the death of Sallie, but it is worth noting that Church, who was only thirty-seven at the time of her passing, never married again. Annette took on the responsibility of rearing Roberta as Church continued with his political career.[6]

Church, heartbroken from losing his wife, immersed himself in work. President Warren Harding took the advice of Will Hays and consulted Church on African American appointments during his administration. As a federal patronage dispenser for the black community, Church helped secure appointments for Perry Howard as special assistant attorney general, Charles W. Anders as collector of internal revenue for the wealthiest district in New York, and James A. Cobb, who was confirmed as judge of the Municipal Court of the District of Columbia. Church wrote letters of recommendation for these individuals, as well as other black leaders who sought federal appointments from the Harding and Coolidge administrations.[7]

Church also recommended whites for political offices. For example, he encouraged Harding's administration to select J. Will Taylor for the post of national committeeman from Tennessee in 1921. Church also had the nomination of Charles B. Quinn, a lily-white candidate for Memphis postmaster, rescinded and replaced by Solomon Seches, whose tenure as postmaster lasted from 1922 to 1926. This appointment benefited the black community because Seches hired local blacks to serve as mail carriers and workers for the Post Office.[8]

Church's position within the Republican Party garnered him national recognition, but it also proved taxing. On a daily basis, Church received letters from African American patronage seekers who sought his endorsement. In this position, Church could remain behind the scenes, but it was not intellectually or politically satisfying. The ingenuity he displayed as an organizer and strategist during the 1920 campaign was limited by his new role. However, the role did allow Church the opportunity to reward the individuals who helped build the Lincoln League into a national organization. Many of the patronage recipients came from a middle-class to elite background, and they had established themselves as leaders in their respective states. Despite their individual successes, they also coveted more prestigious positions within the government. While placing black people in high-ranking federal positions served as part of the Lincoln League platform during the 1920 campaign, Church recognized that this only helped a small percentage of African Americans. The typical black southerner still felt the brunt of white supremacy. Church thus refused to be pacified by his new position or token appointments. Because he had direct access to the White House, he kept the pressure on the nation's highest-ranking officials to protect African American citizenship.[9]

Church advanced the positions of the black community without appearing militant or radical. His correspondence reflects the intellectual debates he had with white politicians on the direction the party should take in reference to the black community; however, he made sure not to offend whites. This approach gave him credibility among white Republicans, forcing them to at least grapple with some of the matters he raised. During the 1920s, few African Americans could rival Church's influence as a leader. He continued to work with the Republican Party and advance the mission of the NAACP. However, most scholarship that exists on black politics in this decade has overemphasized the contributions of people like James Weldon Johnson and Walter White without thoroughly examining the contributions of lesser-known leaders like Church. His name, like those of Johnson, White, W. E. B. Du Bois, Marcus Garvey, and others, was becoming synonymous with black political struggles during the first half of the twentieth century.[10]

By 1920, African Americans made up nearly 40 percent of the population of Memphis. Their support locally for the "progressive" Democrat, Edward Hull Crump, helped keep his political machine relevant. Crump had suffered several political defeats at the close of the 1910s, and by the turn of the new decade the political situation in Memphis seemed to be getting more complicated with the rise of a new political faction. The two political bosses began to work closer together to maintain their stronghold over the local political scene. Crump and Church needed each other because at times either leader could be the dominant political figure in the city. In the 1920s Crump was forced to follow Church's lead as they faced a common foe in the rise of the Ku Klux Klan.[11]

Memphis still had a reputation for being a vigilante town, and in 1921 the Ku Klux Klan reestablished its presence in the city. In November the Memphis chapter, also called a "klavern," marched in the Armistice Day Parade behind a banner that read "One Hundred Per Cent American."[12] The Klan made several other public appearances and started to grow its local klavern, much to the dismay of the Commercial Appeal. Unlike in 1917, when the Commercial Appeal essentially advertised the lynching of Ell Persons, this time the most recognized organ in the Mid-South denounced the Klan and became its most outspoken critic. The Commercial Appeal had once earned a reputation for being one of the most racist newspapers in the country, but in 1922 editor Charles P. J. Mooney took the position of speaking out against the Invisible Empire. In addition, Mooney's editorial cartoonist, Jim Alley, depicted Klansmen being "ordered to unmask, revealing an ugly, distorted face." The caption read, "No Wonder he puts a sack over that mug."[13] The Commercial Appeal continued its attack throughout 1923.

The newspaper's denouncing of the Ku Klux Klan did not necessarily suggest that it had turned over a new leaf. The Mooney editorials probably had more to do with his being a Catholic than the Appeal having some sort of racial epiphany. In addition to Mooney's fundamental religious differences with the Klan, the Commercial Appeal wanted to prevent the possibility of the city erupting in violence. As Mooney noted on April 21, 1923, "Ordinarily the white people and the negro get along very well. It's only when an 'emperor' or a labor agent or something similar butts in that trouble ensues." For their coverage of the Klan, the Commercial Appeal was awarded the 1923 Pulitzer Prize.[14]

Despite its journalistic victory, the Commercial Appeal could not cripple the Invisible Empire. In fact the Klan's presence in the city continued to grow. By 1923 the Memphis Klan boasted a membership of approximately ten thousand. The majority of its membership consisted of "low paid white-collar workers and semi-skilled laborers from white lower middle-class neighborhoods."[15] The Klan had its strongest presence in South Memphis between McElmore Avenue and South Parkway East, west of the Fairground to Barksdale Street, and the Binghampton neighborhood in Northeast Memphis. As scholar Gloria Brown Melton has noted, each of these communities bordered black neighborhoods. These were the same black communities Church had mobilized to the polls in 1920. While a strong anti-Catholic sentiment helped increase the popularity of the KKK, it is not a coincidence that the Klan's popularity peaked after black Memphians played such an integral role in the previous elections. They brought the state its first Republican governor and won the state for the Republicans in the national election. The Klan's power bases suggested the possibility of intimidating these black neighborhoods from voting in future elections, limiting the effectiveness of black leaders such as Church. Other white supremacists took more extreme measures to diminish the influence of Church at the polls, threatening to kill him for his political endeavors. For instance, he received a noosed rope through the mail in 1921.[16] Just as southern redeemers redefined white supremacy in the wake of Reconstruction through violence and intimidation, white Memphians resorted to similar tactics with the hope of disfranchising Church's political faction. This "new and improved" KKK did not rely on mere public demonstrations or squabbles with the media. Based on its popularity in the city, the Invisible Empire entered local politics.[17]

By 1923 the KKK had infiltrated the Memphis political scene, and rumors surfaced that they had formed an alliance with Mayor Rowlett Paine. Speculation swirled around the possibility that Paine had endorsed the candidacy of Clifford Davis for city judge. Davis served as Paine's personal secretary and was a known Klansman who had spoken at several Klan gatherings. Paine had been courted by the Klan before, but he rejected their invitation to join the organization. In order to avoid any further speculation that Paine supported the Ku Klux Klan, he fired Davis from his position and denounced the Klan's activities. Davis responded by accusing Paine of "yielding to his big friends" and joined the Klan ticket for the upcoming municipal elections.[18]

The Klan established itself as a viable political faction within the city. Heading into the November elections, two new parties surfaced. One was the Klan ticket headed by mayoral candidate W. Joe Wood, and another was the "anti-Klan" ticket led by former city judge Lewis T. Fitzhugh. Both

Wood and Fitzhugh ran against the incumbent Rowlett Paine. The three-way race divided the city. Each candidate coveted the endorsement of the two political bosses, Church and Crump. Even the KKK extended an invitation to black voters by asking them to unite as native-born Protestants, a request that the black community rejected. Crump had opposed both the Klan and the Paine tickets. He intended to put his own candidate, Charles W. Thompson, into the race, but Thompson later withdrew. Together, Church and Crump had enough political capital to secure the election for whomever they supported. Fitzhugh believed Crump would support his campaign, although Crump, as late as October 31, publicly stated, "I have had nothing whatever to do with either the Fitzhugh or the Paine Tickets."[19]

Church did not wait to take his cue from Crump. His faction supported the incumbent, Rowlett Paine. Bert Roddy, Thomas Hayes, and George Washington Lee released a statement stating, "The colored voters of Memphis are supporting the Paine administration ticket straight." Paine promised improvements in the black neighborhoods, including streetlights, paved streets, a black policeman and fireman, and the completion of a new black high school. Those leaders declared, "We believe that they will give us a square deal."[20] Black Memphians took a pragmatic approach to local politics. Whites still outnumbered African Americans in the city. Therefore the chance of electing an African American to public office was virtually impossible. The threat of violence and disfranchisement paralyzed the black community. The presence of a black elected official could alone incite a violent response. To maintain the ability to vote on the state and national levels the way they sought fit, black Memphians had to make deals with candidates that could provide their communities with basic concessions. The support of the black community shifted the momentum toward Paine, even though he would never be considered an ally of the black community; in fact a report once described him as "a typical southern Negrophobist."[21] However, he did not represent the Klan, and that made him the best option for African Americans during the election. After rumors surfaced that members of Fitzhugh's ticket had links to the Klan, it sealed the black community's support for the incumbent.[22]

After months of remaining silent, Crump decided to publicly support Paine two days prior to the election. Crump warned that Fitzhugh and Paine would split the white vote in the city, clearing the way for a Klan victory. Realizing that Fitzhugh had little chance of winning, he endorsed his political rival. Paine emerged victorious, polling approximately 12,000 votes to the Klan's 7,000. Fitzhugh received only 3,000 votes. While Crump's endorsement helped Paine run away with the election, the support of African Americans kept him in office. According to Memphis historian G. Wayne Dowdy, "it is easy to conclude that African American voters, rather than the county machine, played the decisive role in Paine's reelection." Despite this victory, one Klan candidate, Clifford Davis, succeeded in his bid for municipal judge.[23]

During this entire ordeal, Church remained mostly silent. He could have been confident enough in his lieutenants and the political maturity of black Memphians that he did not feel it necessary to comment on the contests. Church and the Lincoln League not only mobilized black voters to the polls in support of Paine, but also they educated them on the political process during the previous elections. Therefore they did not always have to look to Church or Crump for direction. They understood the stakes of this mayoral race and responded accordingly. However, Church's silence may best illustrate the contradictions in his political message. As a national leader he had to be conscious of constituents and understand that they watched his every move. It would not have boded well for Church to publicly campaign for a person who had earned a reputation as a white supremacist. Instead, he chose to let his local lieutenants convey the message so that he could maintain his credibility with black voters outside of Memphis. He could not expect black voters beyond Memphis to understand his pragmatic approach to local politics, so in an effort to avoid this controversy, Church chose to stay out of the headlines.[24]

Church and Crump coexisted as the two political bosses in the city. Church's approach to the state and national elections contrasted with his curiously quiet demeanor during local elections. As historian, Elizabeth Gritter concluded that Church and Crum both benefited from their alliance. Church received protection from the police and "could contact city administrators or Crump directly to ask for and secure benefits such as city jobs."[25] Church could deliver votes for the Crump machine and connect Crump with national leaders. Church acknowledged that Crump controlled local politics, just as Crump did not interfere with Church's state and national agenda. As Tennessee historian Lester Lamon stated, "each respected the political power and domain of the other. . . . Crump-controlled local government, on the one hand, rarely engaged in race-baiting and harassment of black political activities, while on the other hand, Church-influenced federal officials seldom interfered with Crump."[26]

Church balanced his position as a local and national leader. Memphis did not have much racial violence, but the southern phenomenon of lynching galvanized national politics during Harding's first year in office. The Republicans dominated the national elections, and black leaders had every right to be optimistic that they would remain true to their campaign promises and make lynching a federal offense. After Harding's inauguration, he declared, "Congress ought to wipe the stain of barbaric lynching from the banners of a free and orderly representative democracy."[27] The antilynching bill that Leonidas Dyer introduced in 1918 gained new life as a result of the hard work of James Weldon Johnson and the NAACP. His bill would hold negligent officials as well as actors in the lynchings accountable; it would also force counties where a lynching occurred to pay $10,000 to the victim's family.

The NAACP worked tirelessly to pass the Dyer bill. Church maintained his relationship with the organization and still served as a national board member and director of southern branches. Associate Field Secretary William Pickens wrote Church, explaining that he would be diplomatic to contact "colored politicians who may have influence with the new administration." Pickens believed it would be an effective strategy for black political leaders to support the NAACP and stand as a united front against white supremacy. He told Church, "If the colored politicians and the colored social workers could speak with one voice and to one purpose, they would be very apt to get what they asked for."[28] Consequently, the platform of the Lincoln League was often very similar to the NAACP's platform. Although they viewed themselves as separate entities, Church's affiliation with both organizations suggests their overall collaboration. Yet the two organizations did not always appeal to the same people. The NAACP remained nonpartisan, and the Lincoln League did not have any white members. By supporting each other behind the scenes, the two organizations appealed to a larger audience without compromise. Their network of influential African American and white leaders increased, and together they would be served as a more comprehensive representation of black America. Church agreed to make the Dyer bill a priority on his personal agenda, as well as on the Lincoln League's platform.

The Republicans controlled the actions on Capitol Hill but remained passive on antilynching legislation. Although African Americans turned out to vote in record numbers and helped place many congressmen in office, they still considered antilynching a nonessential issue. Two Lincoln League officers, Perry Howard and Henry Lincoln Johnson, proposed a compromise that called for "federal intervention only when prisoners already in custody were taken from an officer or from a jail to be lynched." This infuriated the NAACP because they believed that "officials and mobs could easily fabricate conditions to circumvent such stipulations."[29] The organization successfully defeated the Howard-Johnson amendment and continued to pressure politicians to pass this legislation. After numerous delays and accusations from Democrats that Republicans only supported the bill as a political ploy to woo the black vote, the House voted to pass the bill on January 26, 1922, with a vote of 231 to 119. The NAACP's work had just begun, as it still had to fight for passage in the Senate. In June, the Senate Judiciary Committee endorsed the Dyer bill eight to six after a long contested battle. The bill now needed to get to the floor of the Senate, but senators often overlooked the measure to concentrate on items such as labor disputes, veterans' benefits, and taxes.[30]

The NAACP issued a petition that numerous governors, mayors, college presidents and faculty, editors, lawyers, and others signed in an effort to urge the Senate to pass the legislation. When the bill finally made it to the Senate floor, southern senators organized a filibuster that prevented the passing of the legislation. Republicans did not mount much of an effort to counter the filibuster and eventually voted to abandon the Dyer bill.[31]

African Americans had yet another reason to distrust the GOP and withdraw their support for the party. Their frustrations continued to mount because they knew that, if Republicans had brought the bill to a vote, it would have passed. Instead Republicans emerged as cowards and liars in the eyes of the black community. "I think disgust was the dominant emotion. What I had for a week been sensing would happen—the betrayal of the bill by Republican leaders—had happened," reflected James Weldon Johnson.[32] Although the bill failed, the NAACP and other leaders effectively raised the nation's awareness of lynchings. Ultimately, the activism of African Americans during this antilynching crusade helped to curb its practice during the 1930s and 1940s.

In the aftermath of the Dyer bill letdown, black voters began to reassess their loyalty to the GOP. African Americans did not have a strong advocate within the Harding and Coolidge administrations. Black people did not represent the same voting bloc as they did in the 1920 election. The Great Migration was moving black people from their rural communities to metropolitan areas in the South, as well as to the North. In these areas the Democrats developed strategies to appeal to black migrants. Church once again found himself in the position of convincing African Americans that, even though the GOP had repeatedly failed the black community, it represented the best political option in 1924.[33]

In August 1923, Warren G. Harding died, and Calvin Coolidge succeeded him as president. That same month, the Lincoln League of America announced its annual meeting would be held in Chicago from August 30 to September 1 to announce their support for Coolidge. Church also issued a national call to hold a convention in 1924 to address the "grave political and economic conditions that oppress the people; take action on very important matters affecting our status in political conventions and inquire into a very serious situation now agitating the public mind." That "very serious situation" referred to the controversy surrounding the Tuskegee Veterans Hospital. The government had attempted to prevent African Americans from serving on its staff.[34] After years of black veterans receiving poor medical attention in inferior private institutions, the Treasury Department decided to build a hospital in Tuskegee, Alabama, for black veterans. It also presented an opportunity for the thousands of trained black physicians and nurses to practice, as well as run the day-to-day operations of the hospital. Church supported this cause, once again demonstrating that he was more than a political advocate; he was also a social activist.[35]

The federal government initially promised that the hospital would be staffed exclusively by African Americans. However, the Veterans Bureau, the agency that supervised the hospital, issued a letter stating that all key positions would be filled by whites. This news upset the black community, which became further enraged after finding out that white nurses, who according to an Alabama law could not touch black patients, would be assisted by black maids. Whites would receive professional compensation while the black maids would be paid as menials. The president of Tuskegee University, Robert Moton, emerged as the most vocal critic of the plan. The Lincoln League's Henry Lincoln Johnson and Perry Howard joined Moton in their dissatisfaction with the plan; however, the two sides publicly squabbled over who should lead the hospital. Howard and Johnson may have joined the fight for self-serving reasons, as they saw an opportunity to gain more prestige and wealth. Although the two sides disagreed with the leadership question, both eventually challenged the Veterans Bureau to not just integrate the hospital, but to hire a full black staff. Harding had agreed and asserted that it "will afford the colored race an opportunity to show its capacity for service and prove exceedingly helpful in that direction, provided the success hoped for is recorded."[36] Booker T. Washington's former foe, the NAACP, had a solid working relationship with Moton, and it too, joined the effort. Church weighed in with his comments. He made Tuskegee a priority at the league's annual meeting. The Lincoln League urged President Coolidge "to put Colored personnel at the government hospital at Tuskegee, Ala. Good morals, simple justice and every propriety dictate such a course." The league ended its statement: "Every reason foreign to an insane asylum appeals to President Coolidge to stand by the judgment of his illustrious predecessor."[37]

This battle played out in the national media, prompting responses from white supremacist groups, such as the KKK, that promised violence if any black staff entered the building. The threats became so severe that Moton left town for his own protection. He feared that white supremacists would destroy his campus. However, black Tuskegeeans did not budge from their stance, and as a result of their efforts, combined with the national presence of Moton, the NAACP, the Lincoln League, the all-black National Medical Association, and the black press, the white community acquiesced. A black doctor by the name of Dr. Joseph H. Ward received the appointment to lead the all-black facility.[38]

Coolidge enlisted the help of Henry Lincoln Johnson and Church to assemble the staff. Johnson had left Georgia to take a vacation in the Blue Ridge Mountains of Virginia. While relaxing, he received a call from the president asking him to meet at the White House before he returned home. During their conversation, Coolidge asked Johnson about Church. He then informed him that Church "went to Memphis much depressed" as a result of his lack of support in regards to the "colored question." From there Coolidge told Johnson "that my plan was to have that hospital at Tuskegee run and controlled by colored men." He told "Link," as he was known, that he was upset his vision had been ignored, and he had "taken the matter up and I have men now in the Veterans' Bureau" who would see his plan through. Coolidge then asked Johnson to collaborate with Church to prepare "a full and complete list of colored physicians, surgeons, nurses—indeed a complete personnel composed of colored people for that hospital at Tuskegee."[39] Coolidge specified that he did not want the people from one region, but he instead wanted for them to consider all sections of the country. Johnson asked Church to send him the names of all the "doctors, nurses and other persons that you have in mind" to fill the vacancies. He also asked him to consider the salary of the "Superintendent," suggesting that he start at $5,000 a year. The president of the United States personally went south to seek out the assistance of Church and Johnson to carry his vision into fruition.[40]

The Tuskegee Hospital situation proved that black people could effectively organize and fight their own battles. The Lincoln League met a few weeks after Ward's appointment. The *Savannah Tribune* article covering the meeting discussed the reaction of black Tuskegeans and the league's stance on the Tuskegee ordeal. It commented, "The difficult thing for him [the white southerner] to comprehend is that the Negro has at last learned to marshal forces and fight too." The situation embodies the complex scope of the early civil rights movement; all aspects of the black community are accounted for in this struggle. Local black Tuskegeans did not cower to threats of white supremacists; national civil rights organizations such as the NAACP garnered national attention; the political connections of Church and the Lincoln League made the possibility of having a black staff a reality.[41]

African Americans could mobilize in larger numbers than ever before. Church capitalized on this spirit of activism as he and other members of the Lincoln League encouraged more people to organize and fight for equality. At the annual meeting, members challenged "soldiers of the war to take steps immediately to form an organization of their own, since the organization controlled by their fellow soldiers deny them privilege of assembly."[42] Church and his fellow committee members then pledged their moral, financial, and political assistance to help the soldiers in developing their own organization. Black soldiers began writing the league's officials asking for advice and assistance after reading the article in the *Chicago Defender*.[43] Also during the meeting, the league issued a preliminary platform that called for black public officials from every state, an end to mob violence, and advances in education. The league concluded by charging, "The Lincoln League of America represents a people as ancient as the first story of our country. It speaks no fiery words of hate and brag, but gives expression to the millions knocking at the door of equality in their own land and determined not to take no for an answer."[44] Members made it known once again that they intended to do more than usher black people to the polls. Instead they viewed themselves as a civil rights organization that had the power to give black people the political agency necessary to improve race relations in their respective communities.

In August, Henry Lincoln Johnson, Perry Howard, and Walter Cohen held a private meeting with the accidental president at the White House. The two sides presumably discussed the political and economic conditions of African Americans, as well as federal appointments for black Republican leaders, including themselves. They did not speak publicly about their visit, but they did say that the president was most cordial. Coolidge wanted nothing more than to secure his own nomination for the upcoming election, and he needed to be particularly mindful about alienating the black vote. Coolidge met with the Lincoln League members as a somewhat symbolic gesture because he desperately needed to establish a rapport with the black community. Prior to his presidential campaign virtually no one knew his true feelings on the race question. As a vice-presidential candidate in 1920 he remained silent on the subject. Therefore members of the Lincoln League, as well as the NAACP, seized an opportunity to educate Coolidge on the major issues in the black community and attempt to gain his support. Coolidge's campaign team would rely on leaders such as James Weldon Johnson and Church to create a black agenda, much like his predecessor.

By 1924, Church had become a more well-rounded leader. A news clipping, "R. R. Church, A Leader," stated, "The Hon. R. R. Church, beyond question, has met the full requirements of the race and has proved himself a leader true and tried and safe to follow. He is the most commanding figure today, standing in the forefront of Negro Leaders." The article continued, "The stand which R. R. Church has taken on the side for right, the effort he has made, all give him a seat beside Douglas[s] and Langston, Lincoln and Roosevelt, making him a star of the first magnitude to be loved and by unborn generations of the race whose case he so ably represented and for whose rights he so valiantly fought."[45] He had garnered the respect of not only activists and politicians, but also academics. The father of African American history, Carter G. Woodson, recruited Church to the Association for the Study of Negro Life and History. The "Association," as it became affectionately known, elected Church to its executive council, and he accepted. Woodson told Church, "The aim of the Association is to connect with it men of consequence, who have an interest in the uplift of the race that the work may be popularized in all of its ramifications through this country and abroad."[46] He continued, "The Association believes that you are one of the men to take the lead in this work." Church's star shone brightest during the 1920s. Black and white leaders alike coveted his advice and endorsements.[47]

The Lincoln League planned for the conference to take place in Chicago on February 12–13, 1924, in honor of Abraham Lincoln's birthday. Church, Perry Howard, Roscoe Conkling Simmons, Walter Cohen, and Henry Lincoln Johnson each contributed one hundred dollars to cover the initial expenses. They worked to organize the event, and at the beginning of the new year they began mailing out invitations to members. They also contacted branch organizers who represented forty states, urging them to send delegates to represent the various congressional districts in their respective states. By 1924 the Lincoln League held the distinction of being considered the "foremost political organization in the United States" for African Americans. News of the meeting spread from coast to coast. The *California Eagle* proclaimed that this meeting would be the "greatest political gathering in the history of the race."[48]

On Tuesday, February 12, the Lincoln League of America opened its second quadrennial national meeting at the Bethel A.M.E. Church auditorium in Chicago. A "glittering array of brilliant men and women" packed the auditorium. The session began with the entire crowd joining in the singing of "America," followed by a prayer by Bethel A.M.E.'s pastor, Rev. C. H. Tanner. Roscoe Simmons captivated the audience with his "Address to the Country," where he reiterated the principles of the organization. He told the crowd that the league represented "the equality of all men of all bloods and races, and the joint ownership of the United States by those who have defended it; by those who discovered and developed its resources." He also challenged his listeners to hold the "Belief in the future of the American Negro as an American; determination to remain under the flag made sacred by our blood and fight it out; pride in our achievements that answer to all who revile us."[49]

Simmons had electrified the crowd. He later gave another speech that "was often interrupted by the thunderous applause." Simmons asserted, "all that we are, we owe to the American White man; all that he is, he owes to us; the only difference is that he has collected his toll, but tonight I am here to present our claims."[50] Church led the nominations committee and announced the appointment of Perry Howard to assistant attorney general of the United States—an appointment Howard received based on Church's recommendation.[51] Illinois Senator Medill McCormick and Republican National Chairman John T. Adams served as the only white men to speak at the event. Adams honored Lincoln's legacy and promised to meet with members of the Lincoln League to discuss matters pertaining to the race. McCormick told the crowd that the Fourteenth and Fifteenth amendments had been "grossly violated" by the United States, and he believed, "If we endanger the rights of one American citizen, we endanger the rights of all American citizens." Their speeches endeared them to the crowd, but black people needed more than lip service; they wanted action. The conference attempted to address the following issues: "Migration and Its Political Influence," "Our Political Status," and "Congressional Legislation."[52] For two days members debated and constructed a black agenda that would be submitted to the GOP's national leaders.[53]

Lincoln League officials presented a platform that addressed topics such as "Political Allegiance," where they reaffirmed their allegiance to the Republican Party. They called for league members to "train and educate a race—thirteen million strong—in the spirit of the American government" and to strive "to vindicate the sword of Grant and the pen of Lincoln." The league then asked its members to join the fight in making the "Free Ballot" as "free in Alabama as in Massachusetts." They discussed the issue of migration by recognizing that "Thousands of American Negroes are changing their habitation." They acknowledged that some leaders thought it was unwise to leave the South, but the league made its position clear: "It is the belief of the Lincoln League that it is always in order for people to flee oppression and make it to the places where children can be free and their women enjoy the protection of decent society," and that one cannot expect an entire race to "always bear oppression." Officials stated that the South's refusal to allow African Americans to participate in a government where they paid taxes gave them the incentive to find other opportunities elsewhere. On the issue of "Sex Equality," the Lincoln League assured its women delegates that they believed "in the political equality of the sexes." Roscoe Simmons acknowledged, "Those who make a home ought to be quick to make a Government. Those who give birth to men should be expected to give birth to ideas upon which Government of men must rest." The principles and declarations of the league concluded by invoking the presence of Lincoln again by challenging the nation to secure for African Americans all which "Lincoln died to secure."[54]

After members developed a platform to present to the GOP, the conference concluded with a ball held at the local armory. The list of expected guests read like a "who's who" list of black leaders. It brought a social climax to the political meeting. Among the people expected at the ball were Church's half-sister Mary Church Terrell, Emmett Scott, James Weldon Johnston, James Cobb, Alice Dunbar-Nelson, Nannie Burroughs, and A. Philip Randolph. Many of its attendees not only represented black leadership, but also the black gentry. The attendees adhered to the tenets of genteel performance as discussed in the etiquette literature that circulated in books and newspapers during the 1920s. The men wore tuxedos, and women wore formal gowns. The guests made their entrance in a "grand march" to signal their arrival. The ball allowed its attendees to socialize, mingle, and network with the nation's elite black leaders. The ball capped off another successful conference.[55]

While the Lincoln League had Chicago abuzz, another race conference met in the Windy City. Black Chicagoans hosted the ball that weekend to accommodate not only the Lincoln League members, but also the "All-Race Conference." Professor Kelly Miller of Howard University organized what he called the "Sanhedrin," named after the Jewish council and tribunal. "The Sanhedrin: All Race Conference," met on February 12, the same day as the Lincoln League, at the Wendell Phillips High School auditorium.[56] A mild controversy loomed over the two mega-conferences. Some people speculated that Miller attempted to sabotage Church's meeting, and the leaders of the Lincoln League felt disrespected. Others wanted to know who set the dates for the conference and why they would choose the same day to meet. The constitution of the Lincoln League stipulated that they would meet on Lincoln's birthday for their national meeting. On the other hand, Miller had changed the date of his conference "three times, and only selected Chicago and Lincoln's birthday after the conference of the Lincoln League set the time and place of its meeting."[57] League officials attempted to clear up any rumors that they opposed the Sanhedrin. According to the Baltimore Afro-American, "The officers declare that the Lincoln League is constructive, not destructive, and that it wishes all organizations well." The truth of the matter is that Miller struggled to get supporters for his conference, and may have moved it to Chicago to attract the people who had already planned to attend the Lincoln League meeting.

Regardless, Miller had organized the Sanhedrin in reaction to the friction and rivalries that existed among black leaders, and he saw his conference as an opportunity to bring all race organizations under the same umbrella. He ultimately hoped that the conference would "arouse a sense of unity and race consciousness among Negroes." He "emphasized that the conference must be by and for black men in America, must avoid politics and superficial grievances."[58] He made it clear that he did not want women present at the conference. Over fifty organizations sent approximately five hundred delegates to the meeting, including James Weldon Johnson of the NAACP, Dr. Channing Tobias of the Colored man's branch of the YMCA, and Mordecai Johnson, who later became president of Howard University. The all-male conference met to discuss "all phases of life pertaining to the 'Negro in America.'" The league tried to downplay any friction with the Sanhedrin. However, tension did exist between the groups' two leaders.[59]

Church seemed less than enthused about Miller's conference. In fact, Miller contacted Church the year prior and asked him to attend. Miller wrote, "We beg to request the use of your name as a member of the enlarged committee of the All-Race Conference. It is not only your name that is solicited but your active interest and cooperation."[60] He wanted the conference to be devoid of any political factions, because politics stood as a fundamentally divisive issue. Church disagreed with this approach; he believed that the problems that the black community faced were inherently political. The government had created laws that either prevented African Americans from receiving first-class citizenship, or it refused to pass laws that would either protect or uplift the black community. Church also felt that Miller's conference fell short of its advertised goals. He rejected his offer by stating, "From all indications your movement is factional and falls short of your published proposals to eliminate factionalism among your various groups and make one united pull, and I would not care to lose time in a vain effort." Church clarified his statement by explaining that he thought it was "vain because we cannot hope to pull our groups together with any kind of an initial committee that is unquestionably factional."[61]

Miller's political affiliation is more than likely what deterred Church from joining the organization. Church also enjoyed being in control. He held membership in numerous organizations, and almost always served as an adviser or leader within the group. He believed that he had nothing to contribute to the Sanhedrin other than allowing them the privilege of using his name as an endorsement. By omitting politics, the Sanhedrin would simply serve as an academic outlet for intellectuals to discuss the plight of African Americans, but no real action would likely be taken to uplift the community. Others joined Church in his criticism of Miller's conference. Du Bois viewed the Sanhedrin as "an interesting social occasion" which had nothing worthwhile to say on such "vital questions as housing, intermarriage, union labor and the Klan."[62] Ultimately Miller's movement failed as a result of the issues that he had hoped to defeat, such as jealousy, rivalries, and poor planning.[63]

Church did not usually associate with black Democrats, but his confrontation with Miller speaks to a larger dilemma that he faced heading into the upcoming election. Black people wanted to know which side had their best political interest. As a result of Republican letdowns, it became increasingly hard for Church to justify why black people should remain loyal to the GOP. Harding had done little for the black community, and Coolidge seemed to be even less concerned. Southern Democrats never hid their racist agenda, however. As more black people migrated to the North, they witnessed an unfamiliar Democratic Party that distinguished itself from its southern brethren. Northern Democrats, too, avoided any promises to address the race problem. However, many black migrants had never voted, and now they could vote without any violence or intimidation. African Americans had such little influence in American society that they would be willing to flock to the dominant political parties in their region to improve their immediate circumstances. The transition of African Americans from voting Republican to voting Democratic was a gradual process. Black people moved to the Democratic Party after decades of broken promises by Republicans. No one Democratic candidate convinced black people to switch their affiliations. Years of Republicans constantly reneging on their promises pushed black people out of the GOP just as much as Democrats pulled them into their party.[64]

The four years after the 1920 election exposed the true character of the Republican Party. Republicans could have used their control of the executive and legislative branches to tackle issues such as lynching, but they opted to neglect the demands of their African American constituency. Black voters wanted more than token federal appointments for the black elite; instead they wanted protection from the violence and intimidation they encountered on a daily basis. The aftermath of the 1920 election best displayed the dysfunctional relationship between blacks and the GOP during the decade. African Americans had become a more formidable political force than they had been during the McKinley, Roosevelt, and Taft administrations. Republicans could no longer hide behind the claim that the Democrats controlled Washington as they did during the Wilson years, and make false promises that "things would be different" if they had control. African Americans had enough political capital to hold them accountable. For these formerly disfranchised Americans, the 1920 election epitomized their political optimism. It was the most inclusive election in the nation's history. Church ushered blacks to vote in record numbers, and women voted for the first time. Both races and sexes made their presence known during the election and helped to secure the presidency, House, and Senate for the Republicans. Instead of capitalizing on this new political energy the Harding/Coolidge administration looked to pacify southern whites and appeal to lily-white Republicans. This administration began the exodus of African Americans from the party.[65]

As the Republicans prepared for the 1924 election, they needed to rebuild their damaged relationship with African Americans. They faced new obstacles. The voting bloc in the South had changed as a result of the Great Migration. Black people lived in new areas and had new social, economic, and political options. Black voters could also justify why they did not want to continue their support for the GOP. However, the unfortunate reality for African Americans during the 1924 election was that the Democrats, especially in the South, did not serve as a better alternative. They, too, did not appeal for the support of the black community, and in fact still attempted to prohibit black people from voting at the polls. Black voters found themselves in a political purgatory devoid of any true advocate.[66]

So why vote? Church answered this in the same manner as he did before: because it was their right. By remaining active in national politics, black people could still raise the issues and expose the racist attitudes of white Americans. Voting allowed them to grow their movement, to become more organized, more aware, and more active in the fight against white supremacy. The constant rejection of both parties led to the more militant activism displayed a generation later. Therefore, their actions remain an important step in African Americans' struggle for equality. They were not naive, nor did they support the GOP in vain. By calling the bluff of both parties, African Americans raised the collective consciousness of the nation and exposed its exclusionary practices.

In 1924, Church presented the Lincoln League's platform to Republican leaders. In addition to preparing for the Republican National Convention, Church had been asked to head Coolidge's commission to study the economic and labor conditions in the Virgin Islands. The secretary of labor, James J. Davis, appointed Church to lead a group of six other black leaders to assess the living conditions, unemployment rate, immigration issues, and farming conditions of St. Thomas, St. Croix, and St. John. Their stay would be for approximately six weeks, in which time they hoped he would present information that would aid the United States in its efforts to establish new industries on the islands. Church respectfully declined his invitation and focused on the campaign. He needed to remain stateside to concentrate on the national political scene and another battle with the lily-white Shelby County Republicans at the state and national conventions.[67]

Prior to the meeting of Republicans representing the Tenth District of Shelby County, Church devised a strategy to have his delegation seated at the Knoxville convention. He needed to get some of his men on the county and district committees. Harry True, a leader of the lily-white faction, controlled one of the committees that Church attempted to desegregate. At a state committee meeting, Church managed to successfully submit a resolution that allowed for the inclusion of African American men on all local committees. This gave him the leverage necessary to infiltrate True's faction.[68]

He selected Wayman Wilkerson and George W. Lee to accomplish this task. According to Lee, they "employed all the instruments of flattery, lying, and head-scratching to make the lily-whites believe that they were against Church and bitterly opposed his leadership."[69] True believed their performances and immediately accepted them on the committees. Wilkerson then made an agreement with the representatives of the lily-white faction that African Americans in the district would receive "certain privileges" if they agreed to hold separate conventions and did not aspire to be delegates to the national convention. This agreement violated the principles of the Republican Party. Wilkerson's next move was to get the lily-whites to document their agreement so they could present indisputable evidence at the national meeting. Wilkerson employed "all of the clownish antics" to coax the lily-whites to put their proposal in writing and sign the document. After he accomplished this, Wilkerson broke off the agreement by blaming George Lee for compromising their plan. However, the truth of the matter is that Wilkerson and Lee manipulated True and the lily-whites. Church now had the evidence he needed to carry to the state meeting.[70]

Church, meanwhile, convinced a friend, Congressman J. Will Taylor, to have African Americans on other committees. Taylor owed him the political favor after having him selected as the national committeeman from the state in 1921. Their alliance produced a strong "black-and-tan" movement in the state. The phrase "black-and-tan" grew out of southern newspapers that applied the term to the interracial regular state organizations that were formed after lily-whites denounced their affiliation. The Church and Taylor coalition infuriated the lily-whites. After they realized the full scope of Church's strategy, they aimed for revenge.[71]

At an April meeting just prior to the state convention, Church and his faction arrived early and sat in the front seats of a Shelby County courthouse. When the lily-whites entered the assembly, they immediately confronted Church's faction and ordered them give up their seats and sit in the back. The group refused their demands and remained sitting. This prompted a lily-white leader named Ed Kinney to pick up a chair and hurl it at the black-and-tans. From there the entire courthouse erupted, and a melee ensued. A sheriff was knocked to the floor with a chair as he attempted to break up the two groups. Several men left the courthouse bloodied during the scuffle, and one black person was hospitalized.[72]

Black people would not be subjected to the same intimidation tactics used by whites in the past. The *Pittsburgh Courier* covered the story and included in their sub-headline, "Race Men Declare They Won't Quit." After order was restored, the black-and-tans and the lily-whites decided to have separate conventions. Church would again represent the Tenth District as a delegate to the state convention.[73]

Church discussed the segregationist tactics the lily-whites were using at the state convention with J. Will Taylor. According to Lieutenant Lee, the state committeemen "were so incensed over the actions of the lily whites that they voted to give the Church and Taylor faction two-thirds of the Representation from Shelby [County]."[74] Church also defeated attempts made by the lily-white leader, John Farley, to have him unseated as a delegate. Farley argued that his unseating at the national convention in 1920 signaled the lack of respect national leaders held for Church. The Credentials Committee ignored their request, and Church's faction remained intact. Church was then chosen as a delegate-at-large to the national convention. Church's dominance of the state convention could be attributed to "his standing with the National Party leaders, including the President and some of his closest advisers."[75]

On June 25, Church and his fellow delegates took their seats at the National Republican Convention in Cleveland, Ohio. Melvin Chisum of the *Norfolk Journal and Guide* reflected on the historical significance of the moment when he wrote, "It will be impossible for the historian of the future who essays to write the history of the Republican party to leave out the Colored Republicans and the duties which they have waged in the effort to destroy that political parasite of the southland known as the lily-white."[76] For the first time neither John Farley nor any other lily-white challenged Church's position. Church, however, did play the role of mediator in the contest for national committeeman from Mississippi. Perry Howard faced strong opposition from his fellow Mississippian Eugene Booze. Church helped to construct a compromise that would seat Booze's wife, Mary, as the national committeewoman from Mississippi, and Howard as the national committeeman. Other than that, Church maintained a low-key persona at the meeting. A sub-headline read, "Silent Bob Church." Church said little at the meeting. He just "looked and read a lot." He watched as his cohorts Howard, Simmons, and Johnson took a leadership role at the convention and received the accolades.[77]

The Republicans produced a platform that showed more concern for African American voters "since the one adopted in 1908." Historian Richard B. Sherman observed, "For the first time it explicitly urged Congress to enact an anti-lynching law."[78] The platform also recommended that a commission be created to investigate the social and economic conditions of African Americans and for the "promotion of mutual understanding and confidence." The Republicans attempted to balance their position among black voters and white southerners. They did not want to take strong commitments that could anger either side and jeopardize support.

Although the Republicans included African Americans on their agenda, Church still had to fight in order to gain black recognition within the party. Coolidge's running mate, Charles Dawes, had scheduled a speech in Memphis that summer at a Republican meeting being held in the municipal auditorium. Tennessee Republican leaders agreed to allow African Americans to attend the meeting, but they would have to enter through a "separate door and to occupy an assigned section of the hall, apart from the whites." Church heard of the plans and voiced his objection. He then called Massachusetts Senator William M. Butler, who had recently replaced John Adams as the Republican national committeeman, to make him aware of the plans and ask him to cancel the meeting. Butler agreed and called off the meeting. Church had again used his connections with the party's elite to foil the plans of lily-whites.[79]

Battles between the lily-whites and Church carried on throughout the summer. Farley continued his crusade to block black people from participating at the polls, and Church kept appealing to the nation's leaders to step in and stop the lily-whites' antics. Church, in a letter to J. Will Taylor, said that Farley "is one of the bitterest men alive against Colored people."[80] Church had ascended to a high position socially, politically, and economically, and he could have conceded defeat to Farley and been secure in his own success. However, he continued to battle to secure the principles of equality and protect the constitutional rights of all African Americans.

Yet as the campaign moved on, it seemed that Church did not fully believe in Coolidge and his promises. He campaigned for Coolidge, but not with the same vigor as he did for Harding during the 1920 campaign. Coolidge appeared to be giving a contradictory message to his followers. He valued African American support, but he also wanted to continue recruiting white southerners to the Republicans Party. For instance, in August, Coolidge told a crowd in New York, "Our Constitution guarantees equal right to all our citizens, without discrimination on account of race or color."[81] At the same time he refused to speak out against the Ku Klux Klan. A Democratic newspaper commented, "he seemed to imagine that without denouncing the Klan he can avoid loss of votes by saying nice things about the classes that are victims of the Klan's hostility."[82] This further damaged the reputation of the GOP with African Americans, especially after Democratic presidential candidate John Davis and Progressive candidate Robert La Follette condemned the invisible empire in separate speeches. Coolidge's silence on this issue led African Americans to consider other options, and he never fully gained their trust.[83]

The NAACP refused to support any of the candidates publicly, but its best-known member, W. E. B. Du Bois, finally endorsed La Follette for president. More leaders began to challenge Church's position by encouraging black people to develop "independent voting habits," devoid of political affiliations. Coolidge nevertheless won a landslide victory. On the surface the GOP had decidedly won another presidential election, but they also suffered some disappointments. Their votes had decreased in all of the southern states from the previous presidential election, except in Texas. Church also failed to secure Tennessee for the Republicans, as it returned to a "blue" state. Overall the campaign has been described as dull, and black people remained largely unenthused about their choices in 1924.[84]

The myth of Lincoln was no longer enough to energize the black vote. African Americans did not support Coolidge as they had in previous elections. To them he merely represented the best of the choices available. Church and the Old Guard black Republicans seemed to lose a little faith in the party as well. However, Church continued to support the GOP. His allegiance spoke more to his desire to force Republicans to live up to the ideals of Lincoln, rather than being associated with the party out of sheer loyalty. As Simon Topping wrote, "Church was much too experienced a politician to view the GOP nostalgically." Church's pleas within the party reflected "not only the extremely limited options for southern African Americans, but also the disenchantment of a loyal party member exasperated at what the GOP had become."[85]

Church played a role in nearly every mainstream issue that affected the black community during the 1920s. He balanced his positions as a local and national political leader, and he ventured into being a spokesperson for antilynching legislation and an advocate for an all-black staff at Tuskegee Hospital. During the 1920s Church was at the height of his popularity and influence. His appeal transcended politics. Black Memphians of all classes identified with him. He held leading positions in the NAACP, the Association for the Study of Negro Life and History, and the National Negro Business League. He also led the Lincoln League of America to become essentially the "black Republican National Committee." Behind the scenes, Church worked diligently and allowed many of the stars associated with the black freedom struggles of the decade to receive the glory. Church had very little to gain personally from media exposure, and he must have taken pride in watching others create a legacy for themselves, much like the one he inherited. He already possessed name recognition, wealth, and power. Church did not want much attention, and he never accepted payment for his services. He only lent his time to causes he viewed as worthwhile, and would advance the entire black community. During the 1920s very few people eclipsed the influence of Church, and he epitomized the true essence of a leader during the early civil rights movement.

# Church Must Go

For all the success Robert Church enjoyed, he still could not eclipse the popularity of his half-sister Mary Church Terrell. Terrell, "unquestionably the best known, the brainiest, and most influential colored woman in America," brought more distinction to the already praised family name. During the twentieth century, the two Churches had both become prominent members of the NAACP and the GOP. Terrell served as president of the Women's Republican League of Washington and attended the National Republican Convention in 1920. As astute a politician as her brother, she attended his Lincoln League meeting in Chicago to show her support. Herbert Hoover appointed her as the "director of work among the colored women of the East" during his 1932 campaign."[1] Terrell joined her brother in the belief that the Republican Party presented the best opportunity for African Americans to gain first-class citizenship in America. Like other Churches, she remained a lifelong Republican years after African Americans defected from the party. Even though Mary was over twenty years Church's senior, their careers paralleled each other's. However, the two rarely collaborated on any projects and did not converse often. They occasionally bickered and even had a brief custody battle over their nephew after their brother, Thomas Church, died in 1937. Thomas chose to live his life mostly as a white man and only contacted Church for money. A lawyer in New York, Thomas later married a white woman and had a son, Thomas Jr.[2]

Despite their disputes, it is clear that the two had mutual admiration for each other's work, and both took pride in maintaining the Church legacy. They could always count on each other in times of need. After Robert Senior died, Church continued to correspond with Mary's mother, Louisa or "Mama Lou," as Church and Annette called her. He continued to send "Mama Lou" money as his father often did. Church and Terrell would sometimes write to exchange congratulatory gestures and acknowledge each other for their various accomplishments. Regardless of their seemingly distant relationship, the two could count on each other in times of need, as when tragedy struck Terrell's family in the winter of 1925.[3]

Mary's husband, Robert Terrell, died due to complications from a stroke just before Christmas in 1925. Church immediately sent his sister a telegram to offer his condolences and followed later with a phone call. "It is difficult to describe the effect it had upon me," Mary told her brother to describe how she felt once she received his call. It "stiffened my backbone, revived my spirits, and made me feel that you were concerned about me. . . . I can never forget your voice over that telephone as long as I live. I can hear it now." Church did not attend his brother-in-law's funeral because he wanted to be home with Roberta for Christmas. Mary assured him that she understood and did not want to affect his family's holiday. In a state of mourning, Mary confided in Church throughout the letter. Her husband, who was already paralyzed due to the stroke, had been ill for a while, but she admitted that still "his death was a shock." Mary thanked him for being there for her in her time of need.[4]

As Church did when his wife died three years earlier, Terrell immersed herself in race work after Robert Terrell's death. Although the 1920s brought new leaders into the fold, both Church and Terrell remained relevant. Mary continued to serve as a lecturer on women's and civil rights issues. She played a leading role in Hoover's 1932 reelection campaign. In 1946, at eighty-three years old, she fought a three-year battle to be accepted as a member of the all-white American Association of University Women. As late as 1950 she walked with a cane in a picket line to protest the segregated restaurants in Washington, D.C.[5]

Church still served as patronage dispenser and believed he should name his brother-in-law's replacement. He recommended a friend, James A. Cobb, Howard University constitutional law professor, to replace Robert Terrell as municipal judge in Washington, D.C. The White House obliged and nominated Cobb for the position. This move agitated segregationists in the Senate. During confirmation hearings, Mississippi Senator Pat Harrison opposed the Cobb nomination. Cobb served as an attorney for the NAACP's legal branch. Harrison contended that attorneys for "radical organizations" should not hold judicial positions. In turn, numerous black leaders such as Perry Howard, Emmett Scott, and William Lewis used their connections with influential white politicians to block the efforts of Harrison. Church appealed to the Republican National Committee chairman, William Butler, and later met with President Coolidge to urge the appointment. Cobb had supported Church in his many political endeavors and served as a prominent member of the Lincoln League. Church wanted to repay Cobb for his loyalty. After a stubborn fight, the Senate voted nearly two to one against Harrison's reconsideration, confirming the nomination of James Cobb in June 1926.[6]

With the Cobb saga behind him, Church followed his usual pattern of concentrating on local politics in between national elections. In 1927, Mayor Rowlett Paine prepared for reelection. This time, however, he could not count on black Memphians to support him as they had in 1923. He had reneged on most of his campaign promises to the black community and did not make any attempts to court them for this election. Paine did not hire any black firemen and policemen, and he still refused African Americans general admission at Overton Park. The black community's contempt for Paine intensified after he built an incinerator near the new Booker T. Washington High School.[7] The incinerator also bordered the all-black LaRose Grammar School and the Lewis Amusement Park, one of the few parks that black could attend in the city. Church's protégé and World War I veteran George Washington Lee later recalled that Paine had effectively turned "a fine residential and school section into a dumping ground for the city's filth."[8] Paine had no remorse for his actions against the black community. He officially turned his back on the very same constituency that elected him in 1923 when he urged white Memphians to exercise their right of suffrage. Several black leaders voiced their concerns about his failure to follow through on his pre-election promises, and they raised money for a legal defense fund to secure a permanent injunction to prevent the development of the incinerator. This action infuriated Paine. At an election rally he said, "The unusual activities of the Negroes along political lines, now prevailing in this city; the admittedly large number of illegal Negro registrations, the organization of this Negro political club, its publicly announced demands, constitute a challenge to every white man and woman in the city of Memphis to become qualified voters."[9] With that statement he called into question the integrity of Church and his fellow leaders. An enraged black community demanded that Paine apologize. He refused.

Black Memphians lost their battle in the courts to prevent the construction of the incinerator, but as Lee observed, "its leaders proved that the Beale Street colored people had pride and self-respect and the courage to fight for them."[10] African Americans in Memphis had already demonstrated that they could organize and rally behind their leaders. However, the issues surrounding the election of 1927 revealed a new activist spirit among the city's black residents. They finally had enough. As Lee stated, "the sleeping Negro citizen was finally aroused and lashed into action."[11]

By 1925 the Lincoln League of America had dissolved due to a disillusioned membership and infighting among its leadership.[12] Two years later, Church, Wayman Wilkerson, Dr. J. B. Martin, Merah Steven Stuart, Dr. Joseph Edison Walker, Thomas Hayes, Mrs. Laura Jackson, Mrs. Annie Brown, George Washington Lee, and other prominent black Memphians formed a new black political organization known as the West Tennessee Civic and Political League (WTCPL).[13] Church, "seething with indignation," called a mass meeting in June at the Beale Avenue Baptist Church to organize a plan of action. The WTCPL "sought to establish a plan of defense upon which all minds could meet in united action in order that the burdens of people, their common problems, might be met and overcome." It presented a welcome alternative to the partisan politics of the Lincoln League, especially with black voters' growing concerns with the GOP. Although Church remained important to the NAACP's national office, the Memphis charter became somewhat irrelevant during the 1920s and functioned mostly as an underground institution. The repressive racial atmosphere in Memphis never allowed the NAACP to flourish in the post–World War I era. Across the South, NAACP members "experienced violence, harassment, and economic intimidation from white southerners determined to quell their activism."[14] The WTCPL filled a necessary void and provided an outlet for black Memphians to articulate the problems they faced in the city. Their concerns included unlighted and unpaved roads in the black neighborhoods, underpaid black teachers, inefficient medical care, and lack of playgrounds for children. Lee pointed out that, of the $3,000,000 that Paine had spent improving the city, less than $500,000 went to the black communities. With this new organization, Church wanted to harness the new activist energy being displayed by

African Americans in the city to improve their overall conditions. In 1927 Paine became its primary target.[15]

"Bob Church on the Warpath," proclaimed the *Pittsburgh Courier.* The article discussed the perception of Memphis as a racially progressive, cosmopolitan city, but made it clear that, as it is "bordered by Missouri, Arkansas, and Mississippi," it reflected "all of the colorphobia of its neighbors." The article highlighted the two extremes that created such great social contrasts in the Bluff City: "The gateway to the cotton belt, the center of many railroads, the headquarters of hundreds of important business concerns, the city, for all of its modernity in buildings and business enterprise, is culturally barbarous—a savage in Plus Fours—a Tenth Century barbarian in a Rolls Royce." To combat the racial disparities that existed, Church and Lee started a vigorous campaign to register 25,000 voters for the upcoming election.[16]

The WTCPL unanimously supported Watkins Overton for mayor. Church called on his friend Roscoe Conkling Simmons to speak at a voter-registration rally planned for August. During "Citizenship Week," Simmons and other speakers motivated the crowd to turn out in record numbers. He challenged them to follow Church's lead and to examine his record. "He knocked on the door of authority and what happened? You got a U.S. district attorney. He knocked again and got you a U.S. Commissioner and only recently knocked and you got a postmaster." The crowd left the meeting inspired. The WTCPL increased black voter registration from 3,500 to nearly 11,000.[17]

Lee took the lead in making sure the registered voters paid their poll taxes before the deadline. He launched a campaign to appoint a chairman to each voting ward, a captain to each street, and a representative to each block. Lee, a master salesman from his days of in the insurance business, gave inspirational talks that linked paying their taxes to their duty of upholding the race.[18]

The WTCPL organized African Americans prior to either faction fully disclosing its ticket. Publicly a nonpartisan organization, the WTCPL concealed its support for Overton until a few weeks prior to the election. Crump had already endorsed Overton and his ticket mate Clifford Davis—the same Davis that had run on the Klan ticket in 1923. The Crump/Overton camp recognized the success of the WTCPL's voter-registration campaign and wanted to ensure the organization's support. Crump also knew that the black community was upset with Paine and wanted to court them in support of the Overton ticket. By not fully disclosing a choice, Church was able to broker a deal with Crump. Church met privately with Overton's campaign manager, Fran Rice, and negotiated a deal to secure black policemen, black firemen, higher teacher salaries for black teachers, and admittance to Overton Park in exchange for the black community's vote for Overton. Rice promised he would follow through on their requests.[19]

Crump announced that "99.1 per cent" of African Americans would vote for Overton after Church's meeting with Rice. After Paine found out about their alliance, he resorted to his usual racist scare tactics. Paine called the Church and Crump alliance "the greatest menace to white supremacy in the city since reconstruction days."[20] Paine had taken out a full-page advertisement asking the question, "Shall Crump and Church rule through Overton?"[21] He also had an enlarged picture of Church hanging at his campaign headquarters with a caption under it that read, "Will Southern white men and women allow this Negro man to name the next mayor of Memphis?"[22] As a final act of desperation, he put up "pictures of Church in a car pulled by Watkins Overton and pushed by Ed Crump" to motivate whites to turn out and vote.[23]

Overton succumbed to the pressure of possibly losing the white vote due to Paine's behavior and broke his promises to the WTCPL. Crump contacted Lee and told him, "You let it leak out." He continued, "I'll have to deny it now. Policemen will have to wait. . . . All I can promise you is a chance to destroy your worst enemy."[24] Overton's camp then released the following statement: "We do not favor anything which may create race friction, therefore are opposed to negro police, negro firemen, and general admission to the white parks."[25] However, he did promise "to provide more parks and hospitals for blacks."

Overton essentially promised the city's white residents that he would maintain white supremacy and segregation during his tenure. This put Church and his black constituents in the compromising position of either pulling out of the election altogether and voting for no one, or taking these basic concessions as a minor victory for the black community. Overton's half-hearted promise was a testament to how little political agency the black community actually possessed. African Americans had far to go in order to have full inclusion in Memphis society. They could not be totally ignored, but the election still ultimately depended on the white voters. The WTCPL's support of Clifford Davis demonstrated the few options available for African Americans. It also showed their absolute disdain for Mayor Paine. Church's faction reluctantly compromised its beliefs and opted to accomplish its main goal of ousting Paine from office. For now Church's faction had to be content with gradual progress, trusting that they were making strides that would pay dividends in the near future. Still Church and the WTCPL had much to be proud of. In one summer, the black community more than tripled its voter registration. As a community they became even more unified and organized under the WTCPL.

Despite its success, the WTCPL did not have the universal support of the black community. Black minister Reverend Sutton Griggs declared that the WTCPL was "laying the foundation for a race riot."[26] Griggs, who enjoyed the support of white businessmen, took pride in that "southern blacks monopolized sun jobs," and he feared that the WTCPL would make whites begin competing with blacks for those positions. The city had not experienced a lynching in over a decade, and blacks still had the unique opportunity to vote. Griggs insinuated that African Americans should be grateful for their opportunities and not anger the white community. Lee publicly confronted Griggs, arguing that the WTCPL should also examine the unprovoked murders of African Americans by whites. Lee charged Griggs with being an Uncle Tom and continued to challenge his accommodationist approach to racial uplift. Church and Lee were fully aware of the risks involved with being a black leader in the South. Violence was always a possibility, but both men believed African Americans should press on in spite of the threats.[27]

This danger became even more apparent in November, just days before the election. Approximately one thousand black men and women assembled at a local school to learn about the voting procedures for the upcoming election. As they met, a group of white men, "alleged to be unknown to the police, placed a bomb under the school building and set it off while the meeting was in progress." Though it caused a considerable amount of hysteria, no one was hurt. A few minutes after the blast at the school, another bomb exploded at the New Prospect Baptist Church located on Beale Street when Church was speaking at a meeting, tearing a large hole in the floor of the church. White terrorists had declared war on the black franchise. The *Commercial Appeal* made light of the explosions by suggesting that someone had attempted to play a prank on African Americans by shooting "skyrockets" and firecrackers into the buildings. The city's black leadership declared the acts cowardly and assured them they would not be deterred at the polls. No one was arrested. The local sheriff said the bombs were harmless and may or may not have had any political implications.[28]

Lee headed the new class of black leaders in the city and was the face of the campaign. Church, after being vocal at the beginning of the WTCPL campaign, remained in the background for the majority of the election, although he did endorse Overton. His silence prompted speculation that Church did not support the WTCPL any longer and that he disagreed with the city's new leaders. A local black newspaper dispelled the rumors by explaining, "when the voters followed Lieutenant George W. Lee, they also followed Church, for whom Lee spoke."[29]

Despite Griggs's criticism, and the obstructionist tactics of the white community, the black community still turned out at the polls. Watkins Overton won the mayoral race by nearly thirteen thousand votes. Approximately 80 percent of African Americans voted for Overton over the incumbent. Newspapers across the country credited Church, Lee, and black Memphians with the victory. The *New York Amsterdam* ran the headline, "Memphis Negroes Elect Mayor," and the *Chicago Defender* stated, "Bob Church names Overton as Mayor of Memphis, Tennessee." The *Defender* celebrated that "The election was a tribute to the superb machine-like organization of Robert R. Church. . . . There was not a hitch in any part of the combination and despite the propaganda used by Paine supporters in the closing moments, Church's entire ticket went over big."[30]

One of the most controversial elections in Memphis history was over. "It was a bitter campaign but a great victory," Church commented.[31] He succeeded in removing Paine, the "typical southern Negrophobist," from office. Now the pressure turned to Overton to remain loyal to African Americans. While black newspapers celebrated the victory, they still remained realistic about the outcome. The *Pittsburgh Courier* wrote, "Through the effort of Church and the league, some eleven thousand Negroes were registered and a goodly number of these voted Thursday. Whether or not the mayor-elect will carry out his promise as to dealing fairly and honestly with the Negro citizens is problematical but the citizens, white and colored, have given him the chance."[32]

African Americans influenced local elections throughout the nation. "The recent elections in various parts of the nation show that the Negro communities in the cities are increasingly recognizing their political power and voting with greater intelligence," wrote the *Pittsburgh Courier*.[33]

The article discussed the impact of black voters in various local elections in places such as New York City; Arlington, Virginia; Cleveland, Ohio; Detroit, Michigan; Louisville, Kentucky; and of course, Memphis. After decades of work, Church was witnessing an increase in the black community's political consciousness. A new generation of voters who had never experienced slavery, Reconstruction, or the violent "redemption" era not only took to the polls, but also represented the future leaders of the African American struggle. This group had a new sense of entitlement. They did not have the same admiration of Lincoln or believe it was necessary to remain loyal to a constructed image of him serving as a figurative "Moses" for black people.

Church's loyalty always remained with black people first and the Republican Party second. He wanted to transition the black community's "infrapolitics" into a formal, collective energy that challenged discrimination and secured full citizenship for all African Americans.[34] The informal forms of resistance that always existed in the black community were as important as any other aspect of black activism in America; however, black people could only go as far as the laws of the land would permit. Their concerns needed to reach the halls of Washington, D.C., before any substantive change could take place. By enfranchising African Americans and other marginalized groups, they could redefine the democratic process in America and challenge for gradual reform. They needed to move democratic decision-making from the relatively small white elite and incorporate the political opinions that reflected the spectrum of the American adult population. Throughout Church's reign as political boss of the black community, African Americans used their ballot as a form of protest rather than an endorsement for candidates.

Black politics has always been fundamentally different from white politics by the nature of the two groups' experience in this country. The black community's politics always centered on issues of inclusion in American society, as opposed to expressing their opinions on the typical mainstream political issues. For instance, the Lincoln League of America's platforms concentrated on issues affecting race relations as opposed to taking a political stance on the national economy, foreign relations, or the military. African Americans were willing to affiliate with any political party that was willing to address the race question. They used pragmatism and political expediency to negotiate better circumstances for their community. Therefore by the late 1920s black people began considering their political options to a greater extent. Church and his strategy of enfranchising African Americans had a direct correlation with black people becoming more politically mature and beginning to vote for their self-interest. Heading into the national campaigns of 1928, the *Courier* observed that African Americans "are seeing the necessity of ignoring political parties and the empty appeals and voting for the organization that definitely offers something more than kind words."[35]

African Americans were optimistic about the 1928 national elections. Church engaged in his usual battle with the lily-whites, in particular John Farley. But as black Republican leaders prepared to lead their constituencies to battle in various national campaigns, an onslaught of charges and rumors attacked their credibility. Perry Howard, Walter Cohen of Louisiana, Ben Davis of Georgia, and Church were the subjects of federal investigation for exchanging government positions for cash.[36]

That spring, Church's name was mentioned in connection with the failure of the Solvent Savings Bank. The bank that Church's father founded had merged with the Fraternal Bank to become the fourth-largest black-owned bank in the country. The bank, once dubbed the "Million Dollar Bank for Negroes," collapsed due to corruption and mismanagement of deposits. Bank president Alfred F. Ward, vice president Thomas Hayes Jr., and six other bank executives served prison terms. When the bank closed, it had over $500,000 in shortages. The twenty-eight thousand depositors received only 9.4 cents on the dollar after the liquidation of the bank's assets. In all, over fifty black-owned businesses and corporations sustained losses. Newspapers mentioned Church's name in connection with the bank's failure, besmirching his reputation. The government's investigation of bank records revealed a note for $4,000 made by Church in 1925. Although he had paid the note at its maturity, the local white media attempted, erroneously, to link Church with fraud. Church did not seem too worried about the ordeal. "I have never had any questionable transaction with any bank, and everybody knows that I was not connected in any way with the defunct Fraternal Solvent Bank," his statement made clear. "If I had a note there in 1925, it was certainly paid when due as records of the Fraternal and Solvent Savings Bank and Trust will show."[37] Church never was considered a real suspect in the corrupt dealings of the bank executives. However, this minor allegation foreshadowed the turmoil that he faced later that spring.

One month after clearing his name in the bank fiasco, Church became the subject of a much more severe allegation. His problems began after he had Solomon Seches fired from his job as Memphis postmaster in June 1926. Church appointed Seches to this position in 1922, but after two reported "incidents" that occurred in 1923 and 1925, their relationship became strained. According to Seches, in 1923 Church attempted to lease the federal government a tract of land near Beale Street to erect a service station for government trucks for $18,000. Two other bidders offered tracts of land for more than half of Church's asking price. The government chose the lower bidder. In 1925, Church's uncle James Wright applied for retirement from the post office, but his permission to retire was delayed. Seches alleged that Church blamed him for the delay and forced his removal from office.[38]

Church raised more suspicions after he filled the vacancy by hiring G. Tom Taylor on an interim basis. Taylor expected to have his "acting" title removed and become the official postmaster for Memphis. However, he was fired due to his poor performance. Another Memphian, by the name of George H. Poole, a lawyer, contacted Church about obtaining the appointment, but Church did not grant him the opportunity. Instead the position went to Harry S. New. This appointment enraged Taylor and Poole. They blamed Church and Congressman J. Will Taylor for overlooking them for the position. G. Tom Taylor and Poole accused Church of demanding compensation for the position. Taylor stated that "he lost his job because he refused to give Church $1000 of his salary." Poole alleged that he did not get the job because he would not agree to give Church $2,800 or agree to hire black clerks and carriers. Church characterized their statements as "malicious and false," and he "welcomed a thorough and searching investigation by the Department and had requested it."[39] He went on to make a vague statement that everyone in Tennessee knew why Taylor lost his position, and that Poole was not considered because he could not pass the examination.

Harry New defended Church and called Taylor "an ingrate." New stated, "J Will and Church did more for G. Tom than any two ever did for any man seeking a postmastership."[40] He told newspapers that he had known Church for years and believed in his integrity. He also made it a point to specify that he had never solicited an appointment from Church in exchange for cash. He believed the charges would be proven untrue.

Finally, Church named Edward V. Sheeley, a pharmacist, to the permanent position.[41]

Although Taylor and Poole took their claims to the media, their actions did not prompt a formal investigation. When Sheeley commented, "I am deeply obligated to J. Will Taylor and R. R. Church, to whom I owe my appointment," it raised the suspicions of the *Commercial Appeal*.[42] Farley and the local lily-whites subsequently attacked Church. They indicated that Sheeley was not qualified for the position and that he must have paid Church. Farley rallied to remove Church from the party's leadership under the slogans, "Get Church at all cost," and "Church must go."

The fight lasted until the next year, when a Senate subcommittee investigated the issue. One of the subcommittee members, Senator J. Thomas Heflin of Alabama, read a poem that mocked Church:

> Offices up a 'simmon tree,
> Bob Church on de ground.
> Bob Church said to de 'pointing power,
> Shake dem 'pointments down.[43]

The subcommittee cleared Church of any wrongdoing and approved Sheeley's appointment as postmaster by an eight-to-seven vote.[44]

The subcommittee did not prove that Church accepted money. However, the notion that he might have accepted bribes is not that far-fetched. The selling of federal positions by patronage dispensers had just become illegal, in 1926, when Congress passed legislation to prohibit the trafficking of public offices.[45] Evidence proved that Perry Howard, for instance, took money prior to 1926. After the congressional legislation passed, he made it a point to have his appointees sign a waiver that stipulated he did not receive any cash for this office.

Moreover, black leaders were not the only patronage dispensers who accepted money. What is compelling is that Church, Howard, Cohen, and Davis—some of the most influential black GOP leaders of their era—all faced charges that year. The timing of these corruption investigations does not appear to be coincidental. Heading into the national election of 1928, white Republicans made a concentrated effort to oust black leaders from their party.[46]

Especially telling is the manner in which the Republicans voted in the subcommittee meeting. When Sheeley's appointment passed, seven Democrats and "maverick" Republican leader Robert La Follette voted yes.

The other seven Republican congressmen voted no. The *Commercial Appeal* noticed this peculiarity: "It is an unusual situation for northern Republican senators to oppose confirmation on the ground that the appointment was obtained through the influence of a negro patronage dispenser while southern Democrat senators apparently approve a political alignment by which a negro political handles federal patronage for a Democratic machine."[47]

The patronage investigation led to further attacks on Church's character. The local lily-whites, who referred to themselves as the "Hoover Club," contested that Sheeley paid for his position and continued to challenge Church's integrity. Poole became one of the Hoover Club's most vocal leaders. In a district meeting that Church did not attend, Jim Quinn was elected as delegate to the national convention. The lily-whites were confident that they would be seated at the state and national conventions since they did not seemingly have any African American opposition. However, Church and J. Will Taylor organized a secret meeting around the same time as the lily-whites, electing delegates from their black-and-tan faction to the GOP meetings.[48]

Church, in an effort to avoid the customary confrontation with the lily-whites, chose not to attend the conference in Nashville. The lily-whites assumed that Church had succumbed to the negative press he faced that year and conceded his usual seats at the national convention. The arrival of Church and his delegates at the national meeting in Kansas City, Missouri, thus infuriated the lily-whites. The black-and-tan faction once again challenged to be recognized as the regular Republicans from Shelby County. Church argued that the Republican Party would forever lose the black vote in Tennessee if they did not seat his delegates at the convention. Quinn countered by highlighting Church's battle with federal investigators. He then questioned Church's loyalty to the Republican Party by raising suspicions as to why the Democrats on the committee voted in favor of Church. The Republican Credentials Committee was unmoved by the lily-whites' antics and ruled in favor of the black-and-tans.[49]

After the national meeting, Church had to face another local critic. Clarence Saunders, the founder and former owner of the Piggly Wiggly supermarket chain and the current owner of the "Clarence Saunders Sole Owner of My Name Store" chain, took out a two-page advertisement in the local newspaper to appeal to white manhood in the city. He challenged white Memphians to stand up against the "Bob Church/Crump Gang," and "smash" its power. Saunders clamed, "I am a friend of the Negro—I always been," but he later referred to black Memphians as Church's "ignorant pawns." Leaders in the city who previously remained silent seized the opportunity to try to get rid of Church's influence within the GOP.[50]

Church won another battle with the lily-whites, but it was clear that Republican leaders did not value the black Republicans the same way they had in previous elections. Several factors led to the GOP divorcing themselves from black politicians. Black voters no longer voted blindly for Republican candidates and became more vocal in their criticisms of the GOP, which angered the Republicans who expected African Americans to remain docile and unyielding in their support for the "Party of Lincoln." In addition, the Republicans wanted to increase their presence in the South. This gain obviously could not be done with African Americans alone since they were outnumbered by white voters. However, the lily-whites refused to align themselves politically with their black colleagues.[51]

The Republican candidate for president, Herbert Hoover, made a concerted effort to force African Americans out of the GOP and court the lily-white vote. Hoover and his campaign managers assassinated the myth of Lincoln. Hoover disassociated himself from African Americans and gained a southern following after a political miscalculation by the Democrats. The Democratic presidential nominee, New York Governor Alfred Smith, was a liberal Catholic who exposed the religious bigotry of many southern Protestants. One scholar wrote that southerners hated Smith so much that he "could not have won their support even if he had advocated the re-enslavement of Negroes."[52] Hoover challenged the "Solid South" and realigned the party, only appointing whites to manage his campaign, prompting many black leaders to abandon their support.[53]

In the past, Church had contributed his time, intelligence, name recognition, and money to support national campaigns. He did virtually nothing to promote Hoover as a candidate. The Lincoln League had all but disbanded. The NAACP's leadership openly criticized both parties. Walter White refused to head Smith's "Negro" division, and W. E. B. Du Bois wrote in *The Crisis*, "It does not matter a tinker's damn which of these gentlemen succeed. With minor exceptions, they stand for exactly the same thing: oligarchy in the South, color caste in national office holding, and recognition of the rules of organized wealth."[54] African Americans recognized that they did not have a true advocate in the race—all the more evident after Hoover hired Colonel Horace Mann, a former Klan member and lily-white leader, as his southern campaign manager. The GOP made no apologies for courting white southern segregationists.

Hoover had little interaction with African Americans and never quite understood their plight. He grew up in Iowa, lived in Oregon with his uncle, and went to college at Stanford University. He "reinforced the values of rural, Protestant, white America."[55] Hoover believed that people could achieve success based on personal merit, and that the United States provided equal opportunities for everyone. He also believed that nonwhites were intellectually inferior, once describing African Americans and Asians as the "lower races."[56]

African Americans defected from the Republican Party in larger numbers than ever before. Respected black leaders voiced their disillusionment with the GOP and urged blacks to vote for the Democrats. Approximately twenty black newspapers, including the *Chicago Defender, Baltimore Afro-American,* and *Norfolk Journal and Guide* all endorsed Smith. Hoover's campaign shown some concern because it still expected black people to turn out for Hoover at the polls even though he blatantly disregarded them in his southern strategies. He asked some of the traditional black Republicans, as well as some new faces, to serve on the GOP's Colored Voters Division. However, Church and many other black leaders declined Hoover's invitation.[57]

In a letter Church wrote to Hubert Work, Republican National Committee chairman, he explained his decision not to serve as an executive committee member of the Colored Voters Division: "I am not insensible of the honor. . . . however, I cannot bring myself to endorse either the personnel of this committee or the method by which it was chosen, I am forced to decline the appointment and withdraw from membership thereupon."[58] Church believed that Hoover had chosen to appoint powerless black leaders from states where African Americans did not fully engage in politics. Church stated, "Intimate knowledge of conditions among Colored Americans, of their present state of mind, of their growing self-respect, of the feelings of Colored Republicans who create our majorities in the free states, together with my own experiences in laboring for our party, lead to the conclusion that neither important colored leaders nor the rank and file will follow men who have no votes of their own, whether because they hail from states in which colored citizens are denied the ballot or from neutral territory where disfranchisement is universal." He concluded the letter by telling Work that he was still devoted to the party and a Hoover supporter; however, Church's actions suggested something different.[59]

Church was upset that John R. Hawkins, a black former college president and banker, headed the committee. The Hoover camp had not consulted with him prior to the hiring. Church contested that Hawkins, from Washington, D.C., could not hold the Republicans accountable because he could vote only once every four years. Church knew that his comments would have a major impact once they reached the press. He caused a media firestorm after he sent his letter to the major black newspapers. One newspaper declared, "Democrats will draw comfort from the Church letter, although Mr. Church will not bolt the party. It is another sign of the independent spirit so evident in this presidential election."[60] The *Pittsburgh Courier* ran the headline, "Leaders Look Askance at Church's Stand."[61] Church's stance surprised most members of the GOP. The *Courier* speculated that Church was more hurt by being looked over by the Hoover administration than any discontent he had with these new leaders.

Church responded to his critics the following week. He was informed that Emmett Scott, a political leader and former confidante of Booker T. Washington, wrote the article and attacked his character. Church was not shocked that Scott would write an anonymous article, stating that it was a typical article by the "industrious but elusive author." Church declared, "For thirty years his brick-bats have been hurled from behind the coat-tails of protectors."[62] He reiterated his reasons for declining the appointment, citing that he refused to follow "apologists . . . Even at the request of Hoover." Church would not be a figurehead leader, and he disagreed vehemently with Hoover's company.

Church's public statements and his absence from the Hoover campaign speak volumes about his feelings toward the presidential candidate. Even *Time* magazine did a story on the Church/Hoover saga. The magazine speculated that Church "may require fresh and stronger reassurances that the bleaching of the GOP South" was not motivated by race before he endorsed the candidate.[63] Church did not trust Hoover and still had not publicly endorsed him heading into Election Day.[64]

In the last days of the campaign, Church finally issued a statement that half-heartedly endorsed Hoover. Church took out a full-page ad in the *Chicago Defender* titled, "Why I Am for Hoover." This letter to his "Fellow Citizens" summarized his approach to politics and his frustrations with the

GOP. The letter focused more on the racism that existed within the party than on the endorsement for Hoover. Church highlighted the aspirations he had for Republicans, as well as his disappointments. He explains, "Long have I waged war in your name and for our children. I have fought my engagement where unkind men challenge your citizenship. I have stood where man's inhumanity to man has created an empire of bigotry and *I have known deadly and unrelenting fire. I have fled from no battle.*" Church continued, "To such of our countrymen, whether wolves dressed in the clothing of sheep as wear them under the banner of the *free party* or the brigade of boisterous and malodorous braggarts as we see them in array in the *slave party* . . . I am content to know, with you, that the reaper gathers only what is sown."[65]

Church did not immediately reveal his choice in the "Why I Am for Hoover" letter. He instead allowed readers to understand his reasoning process prior to making the selection. "I write in plain language, not to establish the wisdom of a choice, but to reason it through, since reason alone can hold me up in a day so heavy in disappointments. I wish my thoughts be yours," Church explained. He discussed his personal dilemma of staying with a party that had tolerated segregation, supported lily-whitism, and refused to put black Republicans in office. He reflected, "I must be plain and dodge no issue. As I thought of them I felt as you feel, saying with you, Why should I continue to stand?" Church acknowledged the problems of the GOP, but based on the record of the Democrats, he could not consider the alternative. The Democratic Party was currently engaged in a battle with the Supreme Court to prohibit black people from joining its faction. He then listed the Democrats' record of supporting disfranchisement, unequal education, Jim Crow cars, peonage, attempts to get the word "nigger" in the dictionary, and lynching as reasons why he could not switch affiliations and join their party.

As Church concluded, he admitted, "I am not satisfied with some of Mr. Hoover's company, but clearly do I see in Mr. Smith's company the entire array of gentlemen I know who would deny me life, liberty, pursuit of happiness and a chair car for our women to ride in." He appeared torn in his decision and reflected his own stubbornness as a leader. Within the GOP, Church had always been as much of an agitator as he was a supporter. Although the GOP continued to let him down, Church found "it hard to embrace my enemy, remembering that 'Greeks often bear gifts.'"[66]

He promised to stand "with the Spirit of Liberty against the Spirit of

Slavery." He rationalized, "I may not be able to right wrongs, but, under God, I can protest them. The Republican party offers us little. THE DEMO-CRATIC PARTY OFFERS US NOTHING. . . . Herbert Hoover is the better man of the two." Although Smith had a significant black turnout, especially in northern cities, the majority of black voters still shared a fundamental difference with the Democratic Party and could not bolt from the GOP.[67]

Hoover won a landslide victory over Smith. He succeeded in breaking the "solid South" by claiming Florida, North Carolina, Tennessee, Texas, and Virginia in the election. His appeals to white southerners proved to be an effective strategy, and he had no incentive to repair any damage done between the GOP and African Americans. He did not make any promises to African Americans in his inaugural speech or extend any olive branches to their leaders.[68] Hoover's administration, more that of any other president of the twentieth century, avoided race issues, and it did not make any concessions to African Americans.

After the inauguration, Church made one last appeal to Hoover and encouraged him to live up to the ideals of the "Party of Lincoln": "Hoover will surprise U.S." and be "one of the great national leaders."[69] He reassured segregationists that African Americans did not want to take over the government, but they did expect to be treated equally. The success of Oscar De Priest, who became the first African American to return to Congress in over twenty years, instilled a sense of optimism in Church. He wanted to give Hoover an opportunity to do right by African Americans. However, he also made his displeasure for one of Hoover's primary advisers, Horace Mann, clear and recommended that he be removed from office. Church charged Mann, not Hoover, with trying to eliminate black voters from the party.[70]

About a week after Church announced that "he would devote his life to squelching Col. Horace A. Mann and his attempt to make the Republican party lily-white in the South," Horace Mann resigned from his position as the southern manager. Newspapers credited Church's stance for causing the resignation. Mann also relinquished his duties as the patronage dispenser in the South. Unfortunately, for African Americans this was not the sign of a friendlier Hoover administration. Throughout Hoover's first year in office, he did not send one African American's name to the Senate for confirmation. In fact he did not appoint a single black person to a meaningful position until March 1930, when he reappointed James Cobb as the municipal judge in Washington, D.C.[71]

Church quietly observed Hoover during his first year in office. As the president continued to pass over African Americans for political offices, Church's resentment grew. Republican National Committee chairman Hubert Work's personal assistant sent a letter to Hoover on behalf of the RNC during the spring of 1929 pleading with him to reach out to Church. The letter stated that Church worked behind the scenes with the chairman to prevent the defection of black voters from the party. For his role Work's assistant commented, "no one was more active or gave me more intelligent assistance than Robert R. Church of Memphis, Tennessee." He told Hoover that Church devoted time and effort to their cause and "did some of the most intelligent work" on the campaign. Church was also sent a copy of the letter, but Hoover remained unmoved.[72]

Church was not the only one to notice Hoover's overt lack of respect for the black community. Walter White wrote in *The Crisis*, "Any Negro who hereafter regards him as a friend of his race or as having even reasonable human respect for it, must have proof which is not in the possession of *The Crisis*." He later referred to Hoover as "The Man in the Lily White House." Church would join his colleagues in their criticisms of the president.[73]

Church discussed the sentiments of the black community in a letter to the president in November 1929. "Where their hopes had been fondest their sorrow is keenest now and where they had been led to expect the bread of encouragement they have received the stones of contempt," Church wrote. He informed the president that the black community's disappointment was "universal," and they could not believe a Republican would embrace the practice of disfranchisement and attack their citizenship. Even the administrations of Grover Cleveland, a northern Democrat, and Woodrow Wilson, a southern Democrat, appointed African Americans to federal positions. Church scolded Hoover for excluding "twelve million citizens solely because they do not resemble others in face and feature."[74]

Church, although independently wealthy and famous, shared in the collective experience of being black in America. In his correspondence with Hoover he paid homage to his ancestors for their sacrifices to the country. Church also made it clear that he did not want any personal recognition, but he instead wanted African Americans as a whole to be treated as citizens. He called the president's attention to the sacrifices of black soldiers and explained that their motivation to fight in wars was not only to protect democracy abroad, but to make a better way for African Americans at home. Church believed the $50,000 memorial being built to honor dead African American soldiers was an empty gesture made by the government to pacify its leaders. Church stated, "The dead are safe and their memory is as secure as the story of our nation, but the living are with us to contend for recognition as citizens. Such recognition as they contend for will do more to vindicate the sacrifice and honor the valor of our brave dead than all the monuments loving hands could erect in a country of Congressional indulgence." Church concluded his letter by explaining that he did not want the black community's silence to be mistaken for consent. Church predicted that black people would not vote for the GOP in the next election; Democrats who sought "a shelter from the religious storms of the hour, will leave the Republican party a wreck upon the shores of the political ocean."[75]

Church's scathing letter did not motivate Hoover to change his approach to the race question. Hoover commended the efforts of the lily-whites in Texas, Alabama, and Florida for appealing to its white citizens and embracing independent Democrats. He insinuated that southern African Americans associated with the former black-and-tan parties were no longer welcome in the GOP. Hoover believed the lily-whites would be the catalyst for the creation of the New South.[76] Hoover totally eliminated the ideal of the "Party of Lincoln" for most black voters during his tenure.[77]

Hoover appointed virtually no African Americans to meaningful offices. He voted down a proposal to provide equal spending for African Americans. He refused to give in to the NAACP's request to investigate lynching, peonage, disfranchisement, and discrimination in public accommodations. Perhaps most controversially, he nominated John J. Parker for the Supreme Court. Parker had run for governor of North Carolina in 1920 and described the "participation of the Negro in politics" as "a source of evil and danger to both races."[78] Church, the NAACP, and other black leaders worked against his nomination, and it was ultimately defeated. His support of Parker and the ongoing Great Depression pushed more African Americans out of the GOP and into the seemingly more racially accepting Democratic Party.[79]

By 1931, Church's contempt for the president reached an all-time high. Upon hearing that Church was in Washington, D.C., Hoover invited him to the White House to "suggest a tactful reconciliation" with his administration. Hoover wanted to arrange a conference with Church that would "suit his conveniences." Church simply replied he was "too busy." One newspaper sarcastically wrote that this should be added to Ripley's "Believe It or Not . . . A Negro refused to see president Hoover." Church, whom the writer described as "the most powerful single force, in the negro political and financial circles, in the world," reportedly "lambasted the lily-white leanings of the president" and told an interviewer after he declined the president's invitation that, "Gentleman, I am here on private business, which is taking up so much of my time I shall not be able to avail myself of your offer."[80]

Despite Church's ongoing saga with the president, he still supported him locally during the 1932 campaign, though he restricted his activism to Shelby County. Franklin Roosevelt and the Democratic Party dominated the elections for the next two decades, and along the way they reaped the benefits of the mass exodus of African Americans from the "Party of Lincoln." Church, who remained a lifelong Republican, ironically found solace in that he helped African Americans find their political voice.[81]

Church's influence as a leader had peaked in the 1920s, and he made an important contribution to the general black freedom struggle. Church raised the collective consciousness of the nation to the plight of African Americans to the point where their voice could no longer be ignored. The Great Migration forced the majority of African Americans into urban areas, and they identified with the dominant political parties in these areas, including the Democrats. By the 1930s, the Democrats were more willing to address the race question. Even after African Americans switched their political affiliation to the Democrats, Church never blamed them. He instead blamed the Republicans for forcing African Americans out of the GOP. While he believed that politics presented the best stage to debate the problems in the black community, he also recognized its limitations. Church did not expect whites to automatically see the error of their ways and elect African Americans to offices, but he knew someone had to be an advocate for social change. He embraced that challenge. Church used the national platform of the Republican Party to address nearly every important black movement during the first half of the twentieth century.

Grassroots movements that began in the streets of black communities now had a voice in the halls of Washington, D.C., and Church was a catalyst for this transition. He chose politics as his vehicle for change, just as others used education, economics, labor, and the legal system as their mode to bring about equality. It is their collective efforts and incremental victories that led to the revolutions of the 1950s and 1960s.[82]

Church's ability to use the Republican Party as a civil rights tool changed American politics. His stubbornness explained his loyalty to the GOP. He could never get past the history of the Democratic Party. "Above the platform at Kansas City (the Republican National Convention) hung a great picture of Lincoln, but at Houston (the Democratic National Convention) . . . hung a painting of Robert E. Lee,"[83] said Church in 1928. For Church's generation, the Democrats remained the party that enslaved their parents. In their eyes, the Republicans represented the party of freedom. It was also the party that enabled their fathers to vote. However, as voters became further removed from slavery, they could grapple better with more traditional political issues, because they did not have the same emotional attachment. They did not have to fight against the violent threats of southern segregationists to the same extent that Church and his constituents did. When black people began to leave the South and settle in northern cities, they found out they had political options.

James Weldon Johnson described how the Republican Party did not have the nerve to get rid of the black vote. Nor did the Democrats want their support. "The Negro is literally the bête noire of both parties," he wrote.[84] Church, too, recognized this position, but did not believe black people should just accept being disliked by both parties and remain silent. He used politics to challenge the hypocrisy of the Constitution, teaching African Americans that, if they wanted to bring about fundamental change, it had to be done through the vote.

Church described his political philosophy to a graduate student at Ohio State University in 1935: "Thus far the negroes' political influence has been small," but it was important to keep "an active Negro constituency in the Republican Party . . . to arouse the masses of colored Americans to a consciousness of the potency of the ballot, and use it most effectively." Church understood why black voters turned to the Democrats and explained that he never intended for "all Negroes to be Republicans, but that the majority of negroes become politically alive." Both black Democrats and black Republicans wanted the same thing, equality. African Americans would align with whichever party could grant them more equal standing. Whether it was the Republicans in the South, the Democrats in the North, or Communists in Alabama, African Americans defined these parties on their own terms. Black politics centered on being included in American society. The platforms for black Republicans and Democrats called for the federal government to protect their civil rights in America. Therefore, when African Americans defected from the GOP, Church recognized they still shared the same vision for racial uplift. He admitted that he believed the "Negro is fundamentally Republican, both out of tradition and circumstances," and that black Democrats are "merely back-sliding Republicans beguiled by ephemeral promises, or moved by a childish recalcitrance." In regards to some black voters rebelliously joining the Democrats, Church concluded that he "has no objection to the Negro voter applying the rules of expediency in the matter of casting his ballot." His main objective always remained moving the race forward.[85]

# Epilogue

## The Memphis Blues

"LET 'ER BURN" was the caption under the disturbing image of the Church family home afire. In the *Commercial Appeal*, the eighteen-room nineteenth-century mansion, where Church was born, stood in a veil of black smoke. The second caption in the newspaper showed the Memphis Fire Department extinguishing the fire, leaving behind the image of the house's charred remains. However, the firefighters had not rushed to the scene to save the house that had stood as a monument of black success for nearly a century. Instead, they played the role of arsonists. The Fire Department wanted to test a new fog nozzle being introduced at the National Fire Instructors' Conference. The Church family home was deemed expendable because it was "in a slum clearance area." Over "1,400 visiting fire prevention experts and several thousand spectators" watched as flames leapt fifteen to twenty feet in the air.[1] Firemen then surrounded the house and "snuffed it out in a matter of seconds." The roughly two-inch nozzle created a fog-like blanket of steam vapor to quickly smother the flames. The Fire Department used about 9,000 gallons instead of the nearly 75,000 gallons normally used to extinguish a fire of that magnitude. For the firefighters, the fog-nozzle technique was deemed a success while the black community watched as water trickled from the ruins.[2]

Boss Crump authorized the burning of the Church residence as an attempt to not only "test" the new equipment, but more importantly to erase the family's legacy from the city. He hated Church for all that he had accomplished, and he did not want any reminders of his black contemporary. Church served as a delegate from Tennessee at eight consecutive Republican national conventions from 1912 to 1940. His mentee, George Washington Lee, estimated that Church was responsible for the federal appointments of more African Americans than any other "colored American" in history, with the possible exception of Booker T. Washington. In Memphis, very few African Americans exceeded his popularity. "Thousands of them had never seen him in person," wrote Walter Adkins. "An equal number have never had an occasion for personal contact. Many have dealt with him only to become more deeply impressed, and depart to increase with their comment his mythical importance." The black community appreciated his consistency as a leader. He did not present himself as an expert on all issues in the black community, but he supported those who seemed genuine in the pursuit of equality. Church's political perspective centered on the idea of moving the race forward, and he put all of his energies into this cause. Even though he made mistakes along the way, his intentions cannot be questioned. Church's devotion to negotiating better opportunities for African Americans won the admiration of his supporters and enraged his enemies.[3]

The 1930s and 1940s presented new challenges for Church. He faced personal, economic, and professional hardships throughout the decade. The Lincoln League disbanded, and Church never campaigned for the GOP as vigorously as he did in the 1920s. His relationship with Boss Crump became strained during the Democrats' twenty-year reign in Washington, D.C. Yet through it all, Church remained resilient. He did not allow his personal setbacks or the ongoing migration of African Americans to the Democratic Party to discourage his outlook on the political scene. In fact, he viewed the current political trend with an "appreciative eye." Although he remained an admired leader, his relevance began to fade, as witnessed in his diminished role as a federal patronage dispenser. Church strategically used his position to place individuals, white or black, in positions that would benefit the black community. For example, during the 1920s nearly 80 percent of Memphis's mail carriers were black, thanks to Church's ability to select postmasters in the area. By the 1930s, whites regained the majority. His diminished role in the city prompted more unwarranted attacks on his character than he had ever experienced. Local whites forgot about previous relationships they had established as they too worked to undermine him as a leader.[4]

Church had his fair share of racist encounters throughout his career, but they usually revolved around politics. He had avoided much of the typical day-to-day racism that the majority of black people faced, dating back to his childhood, when his father went to extreme lengths to protect him from any form of Jim Crow. An incident that demonstrates Church's waning influence in Memphis occurred in July 1933. Two white motorcycle policemen pulled Church over for driving recklessly down Mississippi Avenue in Memphis. Church took exception with the two officers and expressed his discontent. The policemen then told Church that "he thought he was hard boiled," or superior to them, and arrested him. Church was later released on his own recognizance, and a hearing was scheduled for later that week. In court, the assistant city attorney, Julius Alperin, asked for the case to be dismissed due to the officers' mismanagement of the situation. Commissioner Clifford Davis, who Church had previously campaigned for to become city judge, stated based on an investigation that Church had not been driving recklessly. The policemen admitted that they did recognize Church and refused to repeat the statements they made to him during the arrest after they learned of his identity. The court threw the case out, and the officers were said to have made a "boneheaded play." Regardless of the police officers' intentions, his arrest would prove to be a sign of more bad times to come in his hometown.[5]

Whites seized the opportunity to curb Church's power locally during the FDR years. John McCall, who lost as the Republican candidate for governor in 1932, issued a statement that he intended to "rid the people of Tennessee and the Republican party of the iniquitous influence of Bob Church, and to take from his hand the power to again betray the Republican Party as he has done so many times in the past."[6] McCall threatened not to run again in the Republican primary for governor if Church won recognition at the upcoming state convention. At the convention, in Chattanooga, white Republicans "nailed Bob Church to the Cross," continuing their attacks on him.[7] Local whites felt more comfortable in their criticisms of the former "roving dictator of the Lincoln belt." Although Church maintained relationships with the elite white leaders of the GOP, it meant little locally since the Democrats held the power in Washington, D.C. In previous Republican administrations, Church had been able to use his connections with national policy-makers to secure basic concessions for his fellow black and white colleagues. He could help Republicans that were somewhat sympathetic to the causes of the Democrats. Church no longer had this ability during the FDR years and became useless to the white Democrats who had tolerated him during his most influential years. Church managed to fight off the lily-whites and maintain control of the Shelby County Republicans throughout the decade; however, his position had little impact on the city.[8]

His adverse relationship with the white community could be an expected consequence of his diminished role as a national leader. However, his refusal to leave the GOP influenced his relationship with the black community and most notably the NAACP. Walter White had just been named the executive secretary of the NAACP in 1931. White's contribution to the early civil rights movement cannot be overstated, but his abrasive personality caused conflict within the organization.

W. E. B. Du Bois served as his most vocal critic despite, ironically, recruiting White to the organization. Du Bois expressed his dislike for him soon after White joined the NAACP staff in 1918. When Johnson stepped down from his position as field secretary, Du Bois courted Roy Wilkins, then the editor of the *Kansas City Call*, to replace Johnson as the head of the NAACP. Despite Du Bois's effort, the NAACP Board of Directors named White to the position. Almost immediately after his hiring, the two ego-driven leaders argued about the direction of *The Crisis*. Du Bois began writing about achieving self-sufficiency through segregation, and White was a full supporter of integration. This conflict led Du Bois to suggest that White's views on integration reflected his own self-hatred and publicly criticized his relationship with the Roosevelts. Members of the NAACP Executive Board then censured Du Bois and created a rule that forbade paid NAACP officers from writing critical articles about the organization. Du Bois could not have his voice silenced and resigned from the NAACP in 1934. Du Bois, who had his share of personality flaws, would not be alone in his rivalry with White.[9]

Church had a good relationship with White that dated back to when White stayed at Church's home to investigate the Ell Persons lynching. The two corresponded regularly and collaborated on several NAACP projects, but Church disliked how White inherited his position. Church believed that NAACP executives had mistreated his friend James Weldon Johnson and forced him to resign. At the time Church still held a position on the board of directors. In reaction to Johnson leaving the organization, Church sent a letter of resignation to White to take effect at the expiration of his term. He wrote White in January 1932, two days prior to the annual meeting, to express his reasons for leaving the position. "I was the first member elected to the Board from the South, and I was elected at a time, when the Association was not popular in this section. I accepted the place only because I thought my going on the Board might give courage to other Southern men and women to join the Association," explained Church. "The Association is now a fixture, and I do not see any other helpful thing I can do by remaining a member of the Board." Church ended his tenure as an executive member but remained active with the organization.[10]

One week later, Church reached out to Roscoe Simmons. He told Simmons that he had been a proud member of the board, but "frankly I just got tired of being tied up with some of the people connected with it." Church asked Simmons to write a story about his resignation in the newspaper to avoid any rumors as to why he quit: "The truth is I am out and I want the people to know it." Three weeks later the *Defender* made his resignation public. Simmons mentioned that Church did not leave as a result of the recent NAACP support of FDR, but he did comment on the dismissal of Johnson. By getting his story out first, Church thought he had avoided any controversies. However, White took exception with a comment that Church made about Johnson and published a rebuttal the following week. Usually when Church went to the papers, he did not have to worry about his detractors challenging him, especially in the *Chicago Defender*. However, it was a new day and White had ascended to the top of black leadership by the 1930s. He wanted to protect the reputation of the NAACP.[11]

Under the headline "Mr. White Objects," the head of the NAACP asked that the newspaper issue a correction in regard to Church's reasoning for leaving the organization. He prefaced his statement by saying he wanted to address the article from two weeks ago because it did an "injustice to my friend, Robert R. Church of Memphis, and, by implication, does harm to James Weldon Johnson and to the NAACP." He stated that Church's resignation had nothing to do with the controversial John J. Parker confirmation case or his connection with the white senators that voted for Parker. White explained that Church had not been able to attend the board meetings in a number of years. He then notified the public that the board recommended that his place be filled by newspaper editor William Allen White: "The association's activities in no way entered into Mr. Church's decision so far as we know."[12]

Church countered with a letter addressed "Mr. Walter White, etc." Church told White that he found his article in the *Defender* interesting in view of the facts. "Maybe I ought to appreciate the spirit of it, but I am confused by its discrepancies," wrote Church. White's commentary suggested that the NAACP's executive members had already made the decision to remove Church from the board of directors and named his replacement prior to his resignation. The letters he received from the organization's officials, including Treasurer Mary White Ovington, expressed their gratitude for his service. Church believed that White wanted to skew the facts to protect the image of the NAACP. The perception that one of the primary persons who built the NAACP into the preeminent civil rights organization had been ousted could be damaging to the organization's public image.[13]

Church felt betrayed by White and other members of the NAACP. He told Simmons, "no one has ever intimated to me that my name had been questioned." Church questioned the validity of White's story. He believed that White was only reacting to Church's initial comments in the *Defender.* White then wrote Church again and declared, "Perhaps our letter to the *Chicago Defender* was not clear." White explained once more that he wanted to clear up the implication that Church resigned from the NAACP due to personal grievances. Church shared the letter with Simmons and stated that Walter White's intentions were perfectly clear: "he wanted to convey one idea . . . that William White was elected before I resigned." He then warned that, if White went to the *Defender* again, then he would publish all of the letters that White wrote him expressing his regrets for Church's resignation. James Weldon Johnson told Church in Nashville that he did not know anything about him being replaced, but he thought that White "wanted to get some more publicity on the Parker case." Regardless of White's intentions, Church made it a point in his letters to highlight his accomplishments within the organization. In many ways Church's letters reflect a leader in transition. He seemed to struggle with the idea that the NAACP executives did not do more to convince him to stay. So he became somewhat defensive and grew consumed with protecting his legacy. Church's fallout with White stood as a turning point in his career.[14]

However, the White controversy would pale in comparison to his dispute with Boss Crump. For years Bob Church supplied the "brown screws in the Crump Machine." Church played a vital role not only because of his influence among black Memphians, but also due to his connections with national Republicans. As a patronage dispenser, Church had the power to appoint local Republicans who had sensitivity toward the Democrats. "A hostile federal judge o[r] district attorney could make life very unpleasant for the Democratic organization, but as long as a friendly Church supervised these selections, the Crump machine could operate with immunity," wrote Roger Biles.[15] With FDR in office, the Crump machine reached its maturity and was no longer reliant on the black vote. Crump had no desire to maintain a relationship with the other boss in the city. Crump's candidates won numerous landslide victories throughout the decade, and it did not make sense to court African American support.

The political situation, combined with the economic pressures of the Great Depression, changed race relations in Memphis. Whites used race violence as a tool to intimidate blacks from pursuing the scant number of jobs available. Police brutality and cases of "negro-baiting" increased dramatically. Prior to the 1930s Crump did not tolerate these types of actions in his city. Once the black vote meant nothing to Crump, it shaped the entire black community. Black Memphians had to eventually appeal to Attorney General Frank Murphy after the police attempted to kill a black union organizer by the name of Tom Watkins. They complained that their basic civil rights and liberties had been violated, "aided and abetted by the city administration and the police force." Robert Church organized a silent protest and urged black people not to vote in the 1938 gubernatorial election in reaction to the increased violent acts against the black community. His protest further strained an already fragile relationship.[16]

The two political bosses reverted to their fundamental adversarial positions. "Edward H. Crump brought to Memphis many of the paternalistic racial attitudes common to the southern white planter class," wrote Biles. Crump embodied the feelings of southern segregationists, but he also took the responsibility of granting black people certain amenities. Crump seemed to look at Church as ungrateful for all that he had done for the black community. He felt as responsible for Church's success as anyone else. When Church organized the informal protest against his candidates, Crump felt betrayed. He then launched a campaign to ruin Church. He found numerous code violations on Church's real estate holdings. As soon as Church made repairs, Crump would find other issues for him to fix. Roberta Church reminisced, "it was one constant thing after another, so that you always had to be spending money for repairs."[17] Crump's political machine had finally matured in the 1930s. Crump, now in complete political control, took an apparent jab at leaders like Church in the city after a local black newspaper approached him about an advertisement. He commented, "I wouldn't put an ad in that paper—you have a bunch of niggers teaching social equality, stirring up social hatred. I am not going to stand for it. I've dealt with niggers all my life and I know how to treat them."[18] For years Crump provided tax exemptions for Church's real estate holdings in exchange for the black vote. Most of Church's properties had been technically delinquent since 1915. Now a disgruntled Crump decided to collect the back taxes on the properties.[19]

The changes that occurred throughout the 1930s affected Church beyond politics. Although the Democratic Party crippled Church politically, it ironically allowed him to be more radical in his leadership style. As he became increasingly irrelevant, Church did not concern himself with upsetting the powerful politicians in Washington, D.C. He could voice his opinion with little consequences. Church had nothing to lose. He recognized that it did not make sense to maintain the facade of a political alliance with Crump, so he officially severed his ties with the Bluff City's political boss. Besides leading the protest against Walter Chandler in 1938, Church openly campaigned for Wendell Willkie, the Republican presidential candidate in 1940, to the displeasure of Crump. Crump hated Willkie after the candidate made comments about how he did not want Crump or other political bosses associated with his campaign. Church did not waver in his support for Willkie, even after the Memphis Chancery Court threatened to confiscate his properties. Church ignored the warning and refused to accept loans to settle his debt. While Church was out of town, the city seized eleven of his properties and sold them at a tax auction.[20]

Church's stance and refusal to accept loans ultimately led to his relocating to Chicago with Roberta and Annette. The machine had finally rid the city of Crump's black political equivalent. Church continued to challenge Crump from a distance through his lieutenant, George W. Lee, but Lee never had the impact that Church had on local politics. Losing properties in the auction, combined with the effects of the Great Depression, caused the family some financial instability, although the Churches still owned other properties in Memphis, Chicago, and Washington, D.C. Though Crump certainly held the upper hand in local politics, he did not remove Church from the city until the second decade of Democratic dominance. Church, for his part, could have acquiesced to Crump's demands and maintained the way of life he had enjoyed when he did not have to pay his taxes. However, he opted to challenge Crump. The black community's native son had finally chosen to bid Memphis adieu and to shape local politics from afar.[21]

Church spent the last decade of his life reminding Republicans that black people had left the GOP due to its own shortcomings, but he lacked the fervor of the 1920s. However, his last considerable effort as a leader can be gleaned from his support of socialist labor leader A. Philip Randolph. Randolph was one of Church's closest friends. Publicly the two could not appear more different, but privately they shared the same vision of securing equal rights for black people. Their correspondence provides a lens into the complexity of Church's leadership style. Despite Church's elite status, he remained sympathetic to the causes of the black masses. He shared a collective identity with all African Americans. Privately, he expressed his anger with whites more vehemently. Church befriended Randolph because he believed in his mission.

Church never tried to convert Randolph to a Republican and accepted his more radical political identity. Randolph communicated directly with, and on behalf of, the working class, while Church used his membership in the black elite to negotiate with the country's most prominent black and white political leaders. Their goal remained the same, however, and they would use each other to create a more representative approach to leadership from behind the scenes.[22]

After Church defeated the lily-whites in 1928, Randolph wrote, "Through matchless courage and inflexible determination you have practically routed the 'crackers' who were your enemies in Memphis. . . . Your work there is truly an expression of the New Negro spirit, and I am sure that all Negroes with pride of race are fully appreciative of this work."[23] Randolph watched his friend battle countless times against local lily-whites and later Edward Crump. He, too, engaged in a public rift with the Memphis boss. In November 1943, he was supposed to deliver an address for the Memphis chapter of the Brotherhood of Sleeping Car Porters, and Crump forbade him from speaking in his city. The Boss told the newspapers that no outsiders would be permitted to speak in Memphis. Randolph then declared that Crump acted like a dictator. "The statement by

E. H. Crump reads like a page from Hitler's *Mein Kampf*," said Randolph. He would later say that Crump was a fascist and that he "out Hitler, Hitler." The nearly yearlong saga was just a taste of what Church endured every day in the Bluff City. Randolph, who did not have to be concerned about feeling the wrath of Crump, took the opportunity to confront him in a manner that Church could not. As Randolph engaged in a war of words with Crump, he solicited his friend's help to start a new movement to protect African American workers.[24]

Randolph wrote Church of his plans to make Executive Order 8802, creating the Fair Employment Practice Committee (FEPC), into permanent legislation. The FEPC prevented discriminatory practices in employment during World War II. In November 1943, he asked Church to be a member of the National Council for a Permanent FEPC (PFEPC). Randolph wanted to ensure that African Americans would maintain the basic right of equal opportunity in employment after the war ended and beyond.

The following year, Randolph officially founded the organization and began his crusade. Church fought relentlessly alongside Randolph for nearly a decade to secure the passing of the legislation. In 1946, Randolph asked Church to set up conferences with Republican congressmen, most notably Robert Taft, to urge support for the legislation. He wanted Church to also get the support of congressmen who would be willing to "break filibusters and committee logjams."[25] The PFEPC also named Church as a member of its board of directors in December 1946 to help formulate plans for the upcoming Congressional session.

Congress stalled on introducing the bill, but in 1948 Harry Truman announced that he supported the legislation in an attempt to secure the black vote. After years of hard work the bill's chances seemed promising, but in February 1949 a Senate filibuster prevented the passing of the legislation.[26] Despite the letdown, Church followed Randolph's lead and continued to advocate on behalf of the black working class. Church reached out to U.S. Senator Henry Cabot Lodge Jr., who wrote back that "it has set back the cause of civil rights at least two years, if not more."[27] Unfortunately, the majority of Democrats and Republicans did not find the measure necessary. The NAACP and Roy Wilkins, who had been ardent supporters of the bill since the beginning, no longer found it a priority heading into the 1950s. A frustrated Randolph wrote Church that, if he "had about a half dozen people as sincerely committed to the fight for civil rights and FEPC as you are, we would get somewhere." He continued, "Negroes especially have go to raise some hell in this country in order to get their rights."[28]

Church challenged Republicans to include the PFEPC on their national platform. Church wrote a member of the Republican National Committee and stated that the "Republican Party promised FEPC in its platforms of 1944–1948. There is no other issue, Anti-Lynch, Anti-Poll Tax, or Anti anything else, at the present time, that the Colored Electorate, are as interested in, as they are in FEPC. To them, it is the greatest issue since Slavery."[29]

Heading into the 1952 election, Church endorsed Republican candidate Dwight D. Eisenhower for president because he believed Eisenhower to be more favorable toward civil rights. Church embarked on a mission to return the White House to the GOP. In order to accomplish this task, he returned to the city that he left over a decade ago. Church had visited Memphis numerous times since Crump forced him out of the city, but this time he looked to reestablish himself as a local leader. He became angry with Lieutenant George Lee for "selling out the race" by supporting the more conservative wing of the party.

He had returned to Memphis "seeking to reclaim his power in the local party."[30] Church stayed at the Lumpkin Hotel on the corner of Third and Vance. On April 17, 1952, he sent Congressman B. Carroll Reece a telegram to express his displeasure that Reece endorsed the more conservative candidate, Robert Taft, for president. He told Reece that there was "absolutely no sentiment here among colored Republicans for Senator Taft." Church explained his position and ended his letter by stating, "I have the satisfaction of knowing that I have told you."[31] He seemed like he was making peace with himself. To the end, Church fought with the GOP's highest-ranking members. Later that afternoon, Church called Thornton Matthew, "the Mayor of Beale Street," from his hotel room and suddenly began to gasp for air.

Matthew heard Church struggling on the other end of the phone and called the hotel office. Frank Scott, a black undertaker, arrived at the hotel and found Church alive but leaning back in a chair. Church, true to his stubborn self, refused to let Scott call a doctor. He collapsed. An ambulance carried Church to John Gaston Hospital, where he was pronounced dead. He had suffered a heart attack, perhaps fittingly, in the city where he had spent practically his entire life. "Robert R. Church and Memphis were synonymous," proclaimed the *Pittsburgh Courier*.[32]

Roberta and Annette left Chicago for Memphis. On April 20, 1952, the family held the funeral service at T. H. Hayes & Sons Funeral Home. Reverend St. Julian A. Simpkins Jr. of the Emmanuel Episcopal Church presided over the funeral. Approximately six hundred people paid their last respects to the political leader. His old friend and colleague Henry Lincoln Johnson read telegrams sent by dozens of people expressing their condolences to the family. After the funeral concluded, Church's body was taken to the Elmwood Cemetery and interred in the family mausoleum.

The "Gentleman from Memphis" had moved from a local leader into the pantheon of black leadership during the first half of the twentieth century. He inherited a life of privilege and could have easily chosen to avoid the problems most African Americans faced. However, he shared in the collective struggle to obtain equality for all Americans. Church's talent made him a national figure. Still, Church chose to remain in the background and let others receive the glory. His career suggests that scholars should look beyond the usual names associated with the black freedom struggle and investigate the local leaders who helped shape their visions and bring it to fruition. Ultimately, his work helped to lay the groundwork for the civil rights movement. Church taught African Americans the power of the ballot. In order to progress, they had to bring their problems onto the political scene. His activism went beyond winning elections for select individuals; he looked to change the fundamental structure of American society through political agitation. Church died doing his life's work. Historians should remember his contributions to the African American struggle.

Despite all of Church's accomplishments, his legacy was nearly erased from Memphis. In 1940, the city changed the name of Church Park and Auditorium to the "Beale Avenue Park and Auditorium," an obvious way to divorce the city from its most prominent black family. The city of Memphis would destroy not only his home, but his office on Beale Street, as well as the Solvent Savings Banks. His daughter, Roberta, would dedicate much of her life to resurrecting her family's name and legacy. She also followed in her father's footsteps in the realm of politics. She, along with notable Memphian Ronald Walter and historian Charles Crawford, played an important role in obtaining historical markers to commemorate these sites and honor the Church family's legacy in the city. The family name has also been restored at the park on Beale. Robert Reed Church Jr. was a giant among black leaders. "He was at all times a party man," summed up Roy Wilkins, and yet, "He never was a slave to party policies. He did not follow blindly. From the beginning to the end he was a critic when criticism was indicated, and a strategist who did not hesitate to press his points upon the powers in the party." Through a long series of battles against Jim Crow, tenuous alliances with Boss Crump and the Republican Party, and leadership of the black community in Memphis, "he paid his way and spoke his piece."[33]

# NOTES

## Introduction: The Gentleman from Memphis

1. Roger Biles, "Robert R. Church of Memphis: Black Republican Leader in the Age of Democratic Ascendancy, 1928–1940," *Tennessee Historical Quarterly* 42, no. 4 (Winter 1983): 362–82. For more on Church's relationship with Crump, see G. Wayne Dowdy, *Mayor Crump Don't Like It: Machine Politics in Memphis* (Jackson: University Press of Mississippi, 2006), and William D. Miller, *Mr. Crump of Memphis* (Baton Rouge: Louisiana State University Press, 1957).

2. *Pittsburgh Courier*, April 23, 1923.

3. W. M. Brewer, "Robert R. Church," *Journal of Negro History* 38, no. 2 (April 1953): 249–51.

4. Ralph J. Bunche, "The Negro in the Political Life of the United States," *Journal of Negro Education* 10, no. 3 (July 1941): 567–84.

5. *Cleveland Advocate*, September 2, 1916.

6. Walter P. Adkins, "Beale Street Goes to the Polls," MA thesis, Ohio State University, 1935, 88–89.

7. *Cleveland Advocate*, September 2, 1916.

## Chapter 1. Growing Up Church

1. *Chicago Defender*, October 3, 1936; *Capital Plaindealer* (Topeka, KS), October 18, 1936. For more on Jesse Owens, see William Baker, *Jesse Owens: An American Life* (New York: Free Press, 1986), and Donald McRae, *Heroes Without a Country: America's Betrayal of Joe Louis and Jesse Owens* (New York: Ecco Press, 2002).

2. *Chicago Defender*, October 17, 1936; *Capital Plaindealer*, October 18, 1936.

3. Annette Church and Roberta Church, *The Robert R. Churches of Memphis: A Father and Son Who Achieved in Spite of Race* (Ann Arbor, MI: Edward Brothers, 1974), v–vi. For more on the foundation of the NAACP, see Patricia Sullivan, *Lift Every Voice: The NAACP and the Making of the Civil Rights Movement* (New York: New Press, 2009), and Glenda Elizabeth Gilmore, *Defying Dixie: The Radical Roots of Civil Rights 1919–1950* (New York: W. W. Norton & Co., 2008).

4. Mary Church Terrell, *A Colored Woman in a White World* (1940; rpt. New York: Humanity Books, 2005), 32–34; Church and Church, *The Robert R. Churches of Memphis*, 3–4. US Congress, *Memphis Riots and Massacre* (1866), microfiche no. 1274, card 4, 226–27, Library of Congress. Green Polonius Hamilton, *The Bright Side of Memphis: A Compendium of Information Concerning the Colored People of Memphis, Tennessee* (Memphis: n.p., 1908), 99–100; Roberta Church, Charles Crawford, and Ronald Walter, eds., *Nineteenth Century Memphis Families of Color 1850–1900* (Memphis: Murdock Printing Co., 1987), 16; Clarence L. Kelly, "Robert R. Church, A Negro Tennessean, In Republican State and National Politics from 1912–1932," MA thesis, Tennessee Agricultural and Industrial State University, 1954, 5–6. Clarence Kelly corresponded with Robert Church Jr. while researching his thesis. Their correspondence can be found in the Roberta Church Collection in the Memphis and Shelby County Room of the Benjamin L. Hooks Public Library, Memphis. Deborah Gray White, *Ar'n't I a Woman? Female Slaves in the Plantation South* (New York: W. W. Norton and Co., 1985), discusses the plight of enslaved African American women being sexually abused on the plantation in greater detail. Church and Church, *The Robert R. Churches of Memphis*, 5. The story of Emmeline is mentioned several times throughout the Robert R. Church Family Papers, Mississippi Valley Collection, McWherter Library, University of Memphis.

5. Willard B. Gatewood, *Aristocrats of Color: The Black Elite, 1880–1920* (Bloomington: Indiana University Press, 1990), 26–27; Church and Church, *The Robert R. Churches of Memphis*, 3–4; Terrell, *A Colored Woman in a White World*, 32–34; US Congress, *Memphis Riots and Massacre*.

6. Jacqueline M. Moore, *Leading the Race: The Transformation of the Black Elite in the Nation's Capital, 1880–1920* (Charlottesville: University Press of Virginia, 1999), offers detailed analysis of the construction of the black elite in Washington, D.C. Lawrence Otis Graham, *The Senator and the Socialite: The True Story of America's First Black Dynasty* (New York: HarperCollins Publishers, 2006), 9–24; Gatewood, *Aristocrats of Color*, 26–27. Also see Willard B. Gatewood, "Aristocrats of Color: South and North The Black Elite, 1880–1920," *Journal of Southern History* 54, no. 1 (1988): 205–24.

7. Moore, *Leading the Race*, 1.

8. Kevin K. Gaines, *Uplifting the Race: Black Leadership, Politics, and Culture in the Twentieth Century* (Chapel Hill: University of North Carolina Press, 1996), 13–17; Jennifer Ritterhouse, *Growing Up Jim Crow: How Black and White Children Learned Race* (Chapel Hill: University of North Carolina Press, 2006), 56. See also Evelyn Brooks Higginbotham, *Righteous Discontent: The Women's Movement in the Black Baptist Church, 1880–1920* (Cambridge, MA: Harvard University Press, 1993); Stephanie Shaw, *What a Woman Ought to Be and to Do: Black Professional Women Workers During the Jim Crow Era* (Chicago: University of Chicago Press, 1996). Higginbotham's and Shaw's studies focuses primarily on African American women;

however, their works also provide detailed analysis on the child-rearing strategies of the black middle and upper classes.

9. Grace Elizabeth Hale, *Making Whiteness: The Culture of Segregation in the South, 1890–1940* (New York: Vintage Books, 1999), 46–51; Moore, *Leading the Race*, 3. See also Leon F. Litwack, *Trouble in Mind: Black Southerners in the Age of Jim Crow* (New York: Vintage Books, 1998); Edward L. Ayers, *The Promise of the New South: Life After Reconstruction* (New York: Oxford University Press, 1992); Harold Rabinowitz, *Race Relations in the Urban South, 1865–1890* (Urbana: University of Illinois Press, 1992); and C. Vann Woodward, *Origins of the New South* (Baton Rouge: Louisiana State University Press, 1951), for comprehensive studies on the development of the Jim Crow South.

10. Gloria Brown Melton, "Blacks in Memphis, Tennessee, 1920–1955: A Historical Study," PhD diss., Washington State University, 1982, 4; Church, Crawford, and Walter, eds., *Nineteenth Century Families of Color*, 17; Church and Church, *The Robert R. Churches of Memphis*, 41. See also Molly Caldwell Crosby, *The American Plague: The Untold Story of Yellow Fever, the Epidemic that Shaped Our History* (New York: Berkley Publishing Group, 2006), for more on the Memphis yellow fever epidemic.

11. Gatewood, *Aristocrats of Color*, 71; Moore, *Leading the Race*, 33; Church and Church, *The Robert R. Churches of Memphis*, 27–36.

12. Hamilton, *The Bright Side of Memphis*, 100; Elizabeth Gritter, *River of Hope: Black Politics and the Memphis Freedom Movement, 1865–1954* (Lexington: University Press of Kentucky, 2014), 17.

13. National Negro Business League Membership, n.d., Church Family Papers, box 1, folder 1; Kelly, "Robert R. Church," 5; Moore, *Leading the Race*, 33–35.

14. Mary Church Terrell to Robert Church Jr., October 25, 1889, Church Family Papers, box 2, folder 1.

15. Ibid.

16. Rutledge M. Dennis, "Du Bois and the Role of the Educated Elite," *Journal of Negro Education* 46, no. 4 (Autumn 1977): 388–402; Gatewood, *Aristocrats of Color*, 247–51.

17. Robert Church Jr.'s Fifth Grade Notebook, November 2, 1896, Church Family Papers, box 2, folder 2. Church, Crawford, and Walter, eds., *Nineteenth Century Families of Color*, 20, 43–45.

18. Kelley, "Robert R. Church," 7.

19. Gatewood, *Aristocrats of Color*, 276.

20. *New York Age*, June 13, 1907; Louis R. Harlan et al., eds., *The Papers of Booker T Washington* (Urbana: University of Illinois Press, 1976), vol. 5: 67; Gatewood, *Aristocrats of Color*, 275–76. Julia Britton Hooks is the grandmother of NAACP President Benjamin Hooks.

21. Melton, "Blacks in Memphis," 8; Kelly, "Robert R. Church," 8; Moore, *Leading the Race*, 33–34.

22. Gatewood, *Aristocrats of Color*, 251.

23. Robert Church Jr.'s Morgan Park Academy tuition receipt, January 14, 1904, Church Family Papers, box 2, folder 7; Morgan Park Alumni Directory, 1926, Church Family Papers, box 2, folder 7; Kelly, "Robert R. Church," 9–10; Church and Church, *The Robert R. Churches of Memphis*, 63.

24. Solvent Savings Bank and Trust Company End of Year Statement, December 31, 1910, Church Family Papers, box 2, folder 16; Church Auditorium Rent Contract, April 18, 1910, Church Family Papers, box 2, folder 34; Hamilton, *The Bright Side of Memphis*, 100; Church and Church, *The Robert R. Churches of Memphis*, 65.

25. Mary Church Terrell to Robert Church Jr., September 27, 1909, Church Family Papers, box 2, folder 31.

26. M Street Ten Year Graduation Anniversary to Sara Parodi Johnson, June 12, 1913, Church Family Papers, box 2, folder 43; Moore, *Leading the Race*, 93.

27. Robert and Sara's Wedding Guest Book, July 26, 1911, Church Family Papers, box 2, folder 38; Wedding Certificate, July 26, 1911, Church Family Papers, box 2, folder 38; W. E. B. Du Bois to Robert Church Jr., August 23, 1911, Church Family Papers, box 2, folder 44; Robert Church Sr. Obituary, August 1912, Church Family Papers, box 1, folder 53; Moore, *Leading the Race*, 38; Kelly, "Robert R. Church," 11.

## Chapter 2. Coming of Age

1. Ida B. Wells to Robert Church Jr., September 9, 1912, Roberta Church Collection, box 11, Robert Church Jr. Correspondence.

2. Booker T. Washington to Robert Church Jr., September 9, 1912, Church Family Papers, box 3, folder 6; see also Alfreda M. Duster, ed., *Crusade for Justice: The Autobiography of Ida B. Wells* (Chicago: University of Chicago Press, 1970), and Miriam Decosta-Willis, ed., *The Memphis Diary of Ida B. Wells: An Intimate Portrait of the Activist as a Young Woman* (Boston: Beacon Press, 1995).

3. Church and Church, *The Robert R. Churches of Memphis*, 43–44; Church, Crawford, and Walter, eds., *Nineteenth Century Families of Color*, 20.

4. *Chicago Defender*, October 26, 1912.

5. Ibid., October 26, 1912; December 21, 1912; February 15, 1913; *Philadelphia Tribune*, June 5, 1915; *Baltimore Afro-American*, June 5, 1915.

6. *Philadelphia Tribune*, June 5, 1915; *Baltimore Afro-American*, June 5, 1915.

7. *Chicago Defender*, February 15, 1913; Darlene Clark Hine uses the term "culture of dissemblance" in respect to the lives of black women who were victims of rape, but the author finds that similar arguments can be made in regard to the black elite. See Hine's "Rape and the Inner Lives of Black Women in the Middle West: Preliminary Thoughts on a Culture of Dissemblance," *Signs* 14 (Summer 1989): 912–20.

8. Kelly, "Robert R. Church," 11; Church and Church, *The Robert R. Churches of Memphis*, 65.

9. Mary Church Terrell to Robert Church Jr., January 29, 1910, Church Family Papers, box 2, folder 1.

10. Terrell, *A Colored Woman in a White World,* 188–89; Rosalyn Terborg-Penn, *African American Women in the Struggle for the Vote, 1850–1920* (Bloomington: Indiana University Press, 1998), 67–68; Melissa Victoria Harris-Lacewell, *Barbershops, Bibles, and BET: Everyday Talk and Black Political Thought* (Princeton, NJ: Princeton University Press, 2004), 181.

11. Terrell, *A Colored Woman in a White World,* 186; Mary Church Terrell to Robert Church Jr., January 29, 1910, Church Family Papers, box 2, folder 1.

12. Solvent Savings Banks 1908–1913, Church Family Papers, box 2, folder 16; "The Negro Bank," *The Crisis Magazine* 23, no. 6 (April 1922): 253–54; David H. Jackson Jr., *A Chief Lieutenant of the Tuskegee Machine: Charles Banks of Mississippi* (Gainesville: University Press of Florida, 2002), 186.

13. Lester C. Lamon, *Black Tennesseans, 1900–1930* (Knoxville: University of Tennessee Press, 1977), 222.

14. Melton, "Blacks in Memphis," 30–31.

15. Lamon, *Black Tennesseans,* 222.

16. Ibid., 223; "Along the Color Line," *The Crisis Magazine* 2 (August 1911): 139; *The Crisis Magazine* 3 (December 1911).

17. Lamon, *Black Tennesseans,* 222–23; Laurie B. Green, *Battling the Plantation Mentality: Memphis and the Black Freedom Struggle* (Chapel Hill: University of North Carolina Press, 2007), 6; Miller, *Mr. Crump of Memphis,* 104; Dowdy, *Mayor Crump Don't Like It,* 13.

18. Green, *Battling the Plantation Mentality,* 13; Hanes Walton Jr., *Black Republicans: The Politics of the Black and Tans* (Metuchen, NJ: Scarecrow Press, Inc., 1975), 121; Melton, "Blacks in Memphis," 37–40; Kelly, "Robert R. Church," 13–17.

19. Beverly G. Bond, "Roberta Church: Race and the Republican Party in the 1950s," in *Portraits of African American Life Since 1865,* ed. Nina Mjagkij (Wilmington, DE: Scholarly Resources, Inc.), 184.

20. Paul Lewinson, *Race, Class, & Party: A History of Negro Suffrage and White Politics in the South* (New York: Russell & Russell, Inc., 1963), 138.

21. Kelly, "Robert R. Church," 13–17.

22. Ralph Bunche, *The Political Status of the Negro in the Age of FDR* (Chicago: University of Chicago Press, 1973); Walton, *Black Republicans,* xiii.

23. Walton, *Black Republicans,* 38–39; Hale, *Making Whiteness,* 15–16; See also V. O. Key Jr., *Southern Politics: In State and Nation* (New York: Alfred A. Knopf, 1950); Richard B. Sherman, *The Republican Party and Black America from McKinley to Hoover, 1896–1933* (Charlottesville: University Press of Virginia, 1973); Simon Topping, *Lincoln's Lost Legacy: The Republican Party and the African American Vote, 1928–1952* (Gainesville: University Press of Florida, 2008).

24. Biles, "Robert R. Church Jr. of Memphis," 364.

25. Kelly, "Robert R. Church," 15.

26. Anna Church to Robert Church Jr., October 26, 1913, Church Family Papers, box 2, folder 35.

27. Bond, "Roberta Church," 182–97.

28. *National Beacon Light*, February 5, 1916.

29. Ibid.; Kelly, "Robert R. Church," 15.

30. *National Beacon Light*, February 5, 1916.

31. Harris-Lacewell, *Barbershops, Bibles, and BET*, 206.

32. Ibid.

33. Robert Church Jr.'s Lincoln League Speech, November 1916, Church Family Papers, box 3, folder 24.

34. Harris-Lacewell, *Barbershops, Bibles, and BET*, 208; Gaines, *Uplifting the Race*, 45–46.

35. *National Beacon Light*, February 5, 1916.

36. Robert Church Jr. to Roscoe Conkling Simmons, February 2, 1916, Papers of Roscoe Conkling Simmons, box 2, Robert Church Jr. Correspondence folder, Harvard University Archives, Pusey Library, Cambridge, MA; *Chicago Defender*, February 12, 1916.

37. Lincoln League, Church Family Papers, box 3, folder 25.

38. Lincoln League Meeting, November 1916, Church Family Papers, box 3, folder 25.

39. Ibid.; Kelly, "Robert R. Church," 28.

40. Green, *Battling the Plantation Mentality*, 35; Lincoln League Meeting, November 1916, Church Family Papers, box 3, folder 25; *Chicago Defender*, October 28, 1915; *Commercial Appeal*, October 22, 1916; Melton, "Blacks in Memphis," 40; Kelly, "Robert R. Church," 19, 28.

41. *Chicago Defender*, October 28, 1915; *Commercial Appeal*, October 22, 1916; Melton, "Blacks in Memphis," 40; Kelly, "Robert R. Church," 19, 28.

42. *Commercial Appeal*, October 22, 1916; Kelly, "Robert R. Church," 28.

43. Lincoln League letter, n.d., Church Family Papers, box 3, folder 23.

44. *Nashville Globe*, February 18, 1916.

45. Robert Church Jr. to Roscoe Conkling Simmons, March 16, October 3, 1916, Simmons Papers, Robert Church Jr. Correspondence folder.

46. Ibid.

47. *Commercial Appeal*, October 21, 1916; Melton, "Blacks in Memphis," 40; Kelly, "Robert R. Church," 28; Lamon, *Black Tennesseans*, 56; Robert Church Jr. to Roscoe Conking Simmons, August 26, 1916, box 2, Simmons Papers, Robert Church Jr. Correspondence folder.

48. Lincoln League Platform, September 8, 1916, Church Family Papers, box 3, folder 24.

49. Robert Church Jr.'s Lincoln League Speech, November 1916, Church Family Papers, box 3, folder 25.

50. *Commercial Appeal*, November 7, 1916; Kelly, "Robert R. Church," 29.

51. *Champion Magazine*, January 7, 1917, Church Family Papers, box 3, folder 25.

**Chapter 3. The Roving Dictator of the Lincoln Belt**

1. Gerald Capers, *The Biography of a River Town: Memphis, Its Heroic Age* (Chapel Hill: University of North Carolina Press, 1939), 207; Kenneth Goings and Gerald Smith, "Duty of the Hour: African American Communities in Memphis, 1862–1923," in *Trial and Triumph: Essays in Tennessee's African American History*, ed. Carroll Van West (Knoxville: University of Tennessee Press, 2002), 231.

2. Roger Biles, *Memphis in the Great Depression* (Knoxville: University of Tennessee Press, 1986), 88.

3. Ibid; Paula Giddings, *IDA: A Sword Among Lions* (New York: HarperCollins Publishers, 2008), 615; Capers, *Biography of a River Town*, 207; Goings and Smith, "Duty of the Hour," 231; Biles, *Memphis in the Great Depression*, 88.

4. Wanda Rushing, *Memphis and the Paradox of Place: Globalization in the American South* (Chapel Hill: University of North Carolina Press, 2009), 44; Biles, *Memphis in the Great Depression*, 6; Amy L. Wood, *Lynching and Spectacle: Witnessing Racial Violence in America, 1890–1940* (Chapel Hill: University of North Carolina Press, 2009), 49.

5. *Commercial Appeal*, May 3, 1917; *News-Scimitar*, May 3, 1917; James R. Sweeney, "The 'Trials' of Shelby County, Tennessee: 'Judge Lynch' Presiding," *Tennessee Historical Quarterly* 63 (2004): 102–27; "The Lynching at Memphis," *The Crisis* (August 1917): 185–88.

6. *News Scimitar*, May 3, 1917.

7. *Commercial Appeal*, May 3, 1917.

8. Wood, *Lynching and Spectacle*, 7.

9. *Commercial Appeal*, May 5, 1917; Margaret Vandiver, *Lethal Punishment: Lynchings and Lethal Executions in the South* (New Brunswick, NJ: Rutgers University Press, 2005), 121; James Weldon Johnson, *Along This Way: The Autobiography of James Weldon Johnson* (New York: Penguin Books, 1933), 317; "The Lynching at Memphis," *The Crisis*, 185–88; Phillip Dray, *At the Hands of Persons Unknown: The Lynching of Black America* (New York: Modern Library, 2002), 231–34. For more on lynchings, see Orlando Patterson, *Rituals of Blood: Consequences of Slavery in Two American Centuries* (Washington, D.C.: Civitas Counterpoint, 1998); Litwack, *Trouble in Mind*; Stewart E. Tolnay and E. M. Beck, *A Festival of Violence: An Analysis of Southern Lynchings, 1882–1930* (Urbana: University of Illinois Press, 1995).

10. *Commercial Appeal*, May 5, 1917; Vandiver, *Lethal Punishment*, 121; "Memphis May 22 a.d. 1917," Supplement to *The Crisis*, 2.

11. *News-Scimitar*, May 7, 1917; "Memphis May 22 a.d. 1917," Supplement to *The Crisis*, July 1917, 1–3.

12. *Commercial Appeal*, May 23, 1917; *News-Scimitar*, May 23, 1917; Sweeney, "The 'Trials' of Shelby County, Tennessee," 111–13.

13. Sweeney, "The 'Trials' of Shelby County, Tennessee," 111–13.

14. Patterson, *Rituals of Blood,* 179; W. Fitzhugh Brundage, *Lynching in the New South: Georgia and Virginia, 1880–1930* (Urbana: University of Illinois Press, 1993), 36.

15. Goings and Smith, "Duty of the Hour," 240–41.

16. Wood, *Lynching and Spectacle,* 2; Patterson, *Rituals of Blood,* 179; Goings and Smith, "Duty of the Hour," 238, 241.

17. Johnson, *Along This Way,* 317–18.

18. Copy of *The Crisis,* May 22, 1917, Church Family Papers, box 3, folder 28; NAACP Papers, "The Anti-Lynching Campaign," pt. 7, ser. A, 1912–55, reel 17 of 30, Library of Congress microfilm; NAACP, "The Lynching at Memphis," 185–88; Sullivan, *Lift Every Voice,* 66.

19. Application for Charter, June 26, 1917, Church Family Papers, box 3, folder 30; Church and Church, *The Robert R. Churches of Memphis,* 68; Goings and Smith, "Duty of the Hour," 237; Sullivan, *Lift Every Voice,* 66.

20. Sweeney, "The 'Trials' of Shelby County, Tennessee," 111–13; Sharon Wright, *Race, Power, and Political Emergence in Memphis* (New York: Garland Publishing, Inc., 2000), 36.

21. *Commercial Appeal,* June 6, 1917; Sweeney, "The 'Trials' of Shelby County, Tennessee," 116–17.

22. Untitled newspaper article, no date, Church Family Papers, box 3, folder 23.

23. Ibid.

24. *Western World Reporter,* November 10, 1916; Kelly, "Robert R. Church," 31.

25. Kelly, "Robert R. Church," 31; *Nashville Banner,* November 18, 1916.

26. Wilson Jeremiah Moses, *The Golden Age of Black Nationalism, 1850–1925* (Oxford, UK: Oxford University Press, 1978), 30; *Time,* February 18, 1929.

27. Kelly, "Robert R. Church," 35.

28. *Time,* February 18, 1929.

29. Ibid., 4.

30. Moses, *The Golden Age of Black Nationalism,* 30.

31. George W. Lee, *Beale Street: Where the Blues Began* (College Park, MD: McGrath Publishing Co., 1969), 251; Kelly, "Robert R. Church," 35.

32. *Chicago Defender,* January 26, 1918.

33. Ibid.

34. Ibid., July 13, 1918.

35. Ibid., August 10, 1918.

36. Robert Church Jr. to Roscoe Conkling Simmons, August 3, 1918, box 2, Papers of Roscoe Conkling Simmons, Robert Church Jr. Correspondence folder.

37. Robert Church Jr. to Sara Church, July 26, 1918, Church Family Papers, box 2.

38. Ida B. Wells to Robert Church Jr., August 30, 1918, Roberta Church Collection, box 6, Robert Church Jr. Correspondence folder.

39. *Chicago Defender,* September 28, 1918.

40. Robert Church Jr. to Roscoe Conkling Simmons, August 3, 1918, Simmons Papers.

41. Marcus Boulware, "Roscoe Conkling Simmons: The Golden Voiced Politico," *Negro History Bulletin* 29 (March 1966): 131–32.

42. Kelly, "Robert R. Church," 36; *Chicago Defender,* October 26, 1918.

43. Sherman, *The Republican Party and Black America,* 135; Will Hays to Robert Church Jr., June 3, 1918, Church Family Papers, box 3, folder 35.

44. Glenda Gilmore, "False Friends and Avowed Enemies: Southern African Americans and Party Allegiances in the 1920s," in *Jumpin' Jim Crow: Southern Politics from Civil War to Civil Rights,* ed. Jane Dailey, Glenda Elizabeth Gilmore, and Bryant Simon (Princeton, NJ: Princeton University Press, 2000), 224.

45. Ibid.

46. Sullivan, *Lift Every Voice,* 61.

47. Robert Church Jr. to James Weldon Johnson, March 19, 1918, Church Family Papers, box 3, folder 31.

48. Robert Church Jr. to James Weldon Johnson, October 24, 1918, Roberta Church Collection, box 6, NAACP folder.

49. Sullivan, *Lift Every Voice,* 75.

50. Walter White to Anna Church, December 12, 1918, Church Family Papers, box 3, folder 31.

51. Copy of the NAACP Branch *Bulletin,* January 1919, Roberta Church Collection, box 6, NAACP folder.

52. Church and Church, *The Robert R. Churches of Memphis,* 68; Sullivan, *Lift Every Voice,* 66.

53. Church and Church, *The Robert R. Churches of Memphis,* 69–70.

54. Steven Hahn, *A Nation Under Our Feet: Black Political Struggles in the Rural South from Slavery to Migration* (Cambridge, MA: Harvard University Press, 2005), 463.

55. Gilmore, "False Friends and Avowed Enemies," 224.

## Chapter 4. We Return Fighting

1. Nan Woodruff, "The New Negro in the American Congo: World War I and the Elaine, Arkansas Massacre of 1919," in Adam Green and Charles Payne, eds., *Time Longer than Rope: A Century of African American Activism* (New York: New York University, 2003), 150–52; Adam Fairclough, *Better Day Coming: Blacks and Equality, 1890–2000* (New York: Viking Penguin, 2001), 104; O. A. Rodgers Jr., "The Elaine Race Riots of 1919," *Arkansas Historical Quarterly* 19, no. 2 (Summer 1960): 142–50; Woodruff, "The New Negro in the American Congo," 150–78. Grif Stockley, *Blood in Their Eyes: The Elaine Race Massacres of 1919* (Fayetteville: University of Arkansas Press, 2001) is the most comprehensive study on the Elaine riots.

2. Rodgers, "The Elaine Race Riots of 1919," 142–50; Tom Dillard, "Scipio A. Jones," *Arkansas Historical Quarterly* 31, no. 3 (Autumn 1972): 206–19.

3. Fairclough, *Better Day Coming*, 105.

4. Sullivan, *Lift Every Voice*, 88.

5. Ibid.; Giddings, *IDA: A Sword Among Lions*, 604; Darlene Clark Hine, *The African American Odyssey*, 4th ed. (Upper Saddle River, NJ: Pearson, 2008), 434.

6. Thomas Price to Walter White, November 26, 1919, Church Family Papers, box 3, folder 31; Dillard, "Scipio A. Jones," 201–19.

7. James W. Johnson to Robert Church Jr., December 2, 1919, Church Family Papers, box 3, folder 31.

8. Ibid.

9. Unnamed Phillips County, Arkansas, detective to the NAACP, November 26, 1919, Church Family Papers, box 3, folder 31.

10. James W. Johnson to Robert Church Jr., October 20, 1921, Church Family Papers, box 3, folder 31; Rodgers, "The Elaine Race Riots of 1919," 150.

11. NAACP 1917–68 correspondence, Church Family Papers, box 3, folder 31.

12. Giddings, *IDA: A Sword Among Lions*, 615; Lynn Dumenil, *Modern Temper: American Culture and Society in the 1920s* (New York: Hill and Wang, 1995), 8–9.

13. Dumenil, *Modern Temper*, 8; David Levering Lewis, *When Harlem Was in Vogue* (New York: Penguin Books, 1997).

14. W. E. B. Du Bois, "Returning Soldiers," *The Crisis* 17 (May 1919): 13.

15. "Race War," *The Crisis* 16 (September 1919): 247–49; Benjamin Mays, *Born to Rebel: An Autobiography* (Athens: University of Georgia Press, 1987), 68; Fairclough, *Better Day Coming*, 102–3. For more on black soldiers during World War I, see Chad Louis Williams, *Torchbearers of Democracy: African American Soldiers in the World War I Era* (Chapel Hill: University of North Carolina Press, 2010); Adriane Lentz-Smith, *Freedom Struggles: African Americans and World War I* (Cambridge, MA: Harvard University Press, 2009); Leon Litwack, *How Free Is Free? The Long Death of Jim Crow* (Cambridge, MA: Harvard University Press, 2009), 46–47; Scott Ellsworth, *Death in a Promised Land: The Tulsa Race Riot of 1921* (Baton Rouge: Louisiana State University, 1982), 45–70.

16. Giddings, *IDA: A Sword Among Lions*, 593; Kenneth Janken, *Walter White: Mr. NAACP* (Chapel Hill: University of North Carolina Press, 2003), 43.

17. Giddings, *IDA: A Sword Among Lions*, 592.

18. Sullivan, *Lift Every Voice*, 89.

19. *Commercial Appeal*, October 24, 1918; Lamon, *Black Tennesseans*, 233.

20. Lamon, *Black Tennesseans*, 235.

21. Lewis, *When Harlem Was in Vogue*, 50–58.

22. W. E. B. Du Bois, "Let Us Reason Together," *The Crisis* 18 (September 1919): 231.

23. Lamon, *Black Tennesseans*, 235; Fairclough, *Better Day Coming*, 103.

24. Gilmore, *Defying Dixie*; Lamon, *Black Tennesseans*, 235; Sullivan, *Lift Every Voice*, 89.

25. NAACP, 1917–68 correspondence, Church Family Papers, box 3, folder 31; National Republican politics correspondence, 1918–29, Church Family Papers, box 3, folder 33; Church and Church, *The Robert R. Churches of Memphis*, 67–86; Kelly, "Robert R. Church," 46–68.

26. NAACP letter to both political parties, June 2, 1919, Church Family Papers, box 3, folder 31; Robert Church Jr. correspondence with Republican National Chairman Will Hays, Church Family Papers, box 3, folder 35.

27. Robert Church Jr. to Will Hays, August 25, 1919, Church Family Papers, box 3, folder 35.

28. Ibid., August 17, 1919, Church Family Papers, box 3, folder 35.

29. Ibid., August 25, 1919, Church Family Papers, box 3, folder 35.

30. Ibid.

31. Robert Church Jr. to Will Hays, August 17, 1919, Church Family Papers, box 3, folder 31.

32. Ibid., October 29, 1919, Church Family Papers, box 3, folder 35.

33. Ibid., no date, Church Family Papers, box 3, folder 35. Also see Walton, *Black Republicans*; Sherman, *The Republican Party and Black America*; Lewinson, *Race, Class, & Party*; Key, *Southern Politics*.

34. Will Hays to Robert Church Jr., December 19, 1919, Church Family Papers, box 3, folder 35.

35. Ibid.

36. Will Hays to Robert Church Jr., January 1, 1920, Church Family Papers, box 3, folder 35.

37. National Republican politics, 1918–29, Church Family Papers, box 3, folder 33; Sherman, *The Republican Party and Black America*, 135–44; Walton, *Black Republicans*, 121–22.

38. Gritter, *River of Hope*, 60.

39. Kelly, "Robert Church," 40; *Commercial Appeal*, January 4, 1920.

40. Giddings, *IDA: A Sword Among Lions*, 615.

41. Terrell, *A Colored Woman in a White World*, 29.

42. Sara Johnson Church, "Voter Registration, 1920–1921," Church Family Papers, box 3, FF 36; Annette Church to Robert Church Jr., June 6, 1920, Church Family Papers, box 2, General Correspondence folder.

43. Terborg-Penn, *African American Women in the Struggle for the Vote*, 145; Giddings, *IDA: A Sword Among Lions*, 615; *Chicago Defender*, February 28, 1920; Church and Church, *The Robert R. Churches of Memphis*, 106. Also see Paula Giddings, *When and Where I Enter: The Impact of Black Women on Race and Sex in America* (New York: HarperCollins, 1996), 119–31.

44. *New Orleans Item*, June 18, 1919, Church Family Papers, box 3, folder 25.

45. Ibid.

46. *New Orleans Times Picayune,* June 18, 1919.

47. Ibid.; P. B. S. Pinchback to Robert Church Jr., June 19, 1919, Church Family Papers, box 3, folder 24.

48. *Philadelphia Tribune,* January 24, 1920; *Baltimore Afro-American,* January 30, 1920; *Chicago Defender,* January 31, 1920.

49. Hahn, *A Nation Under Our Feet,* 4–5; Church and Church, *The Robert R. Churches of Memphis,* 104–5; Gilmore, "False Friends and Avowed Enemies," 220.

50. *Chicago Defender,* June 28, 1919; Church and Church, *The Robert R. Churches of Memphis,* 105; Kelly, "Robert R. Church," 40.

51. *Philadelphia Tribune,* January 24, 1920; *Baltimore Afro-American,* January 30, 1920; *Chicago Defender,* January 31, 1920.

52. *Chicago Defender,* February 7, 1920.

53. Ibid., February 14, 1920.

54. Ibid.; Eric Foner, *The Story of American Freedom* (New York: W. W. Norton & Co., 1998), 97.

55. *Chicago Defender,* February 28, 1920.

56. Ibid., February 14, 21, 28, 1920.

57. Ibid., February 21, 1920.

58. Ibid., June 5, 1920.

59. Sherman, *The Republican Party and Black America,* 133.

60. Ibid., 135.

61. Kelly, "Robert R. Church," 48.

62. David Tucker, *Lieutenant Lee of Beale Street* (Nashville: Vanderbilt University Press, 1971), 73.

63. Ibid., 72–73, 256; *Commercial Appeal,* February 22, 1920.

64. Tucker, *Lieutenant Lee of Beale Street,* 73; Kelly, "Robert R. Church," 52; *Nashville Banner,* April 14, 1920.

65. Lee, *Beale Street,* 258; Republican Nominating Petition, May 29, 1922, Church Family Papers, box 3, folder 50.

66. Annette Church to Robert Church Jr., June 6, 1920, Church Family Papers, box 2, General Correspondence folder.

67. Tucker, *Lieutenant Lee of Beale Street,* 74.

68. Robert Church Jr. to James Weldon Johnson, June 22, 1920, box C-388, Papers of the NAACP, part 11, series B, Harding through YWCA MR, reel 18.

69. Lee, *Beale Street,* 258–59.

70. Ibid.; Tucker, *Lieutenant Lee of Beale Street,* 74–75; Kelly, "Robert R. Church," 55; *New York Age,* June 19, 1920; *The Crisis* 20 (September 1920): 215.

71. Tucker, *Lieutenant Lee of Beale Street,* 75.

72. Sherman, *The Republican Party and Black America,* 137.

73. Will Hays to Robert Church Jr., July 3, 1920, Church Family Papers, box 3, folder 35.

74. Sherman, *The Republican Party and Black America*, 137.

75. Robert Church Jr. to Will Hays, June 16, 1920, Church Family Papers, box 3, folder 35; Sherman, *The Republican Party and Black America*, 138.

76. Sherman, *The Republican Party and Black America*, 140.

77. Ibid.

78. *Nashville Globe*, October 29, 1920; Church and Church, *The Robert R. Churches of Memphis*, 124.

79. Church and Church, *The Robert R. Churches of Memphis*, 125.

80. Will Hays to Robert Church Jr., October 30, 1920, Church Family Papers, box 3, folder 35; Kelly, "Robert R. Church," 60.

81. *Western World Reporter*, November 12, 1920, Church Family Papers, box 4, folder 2; *Wilmington Advocate*, November 12, 1920; Church and Church, *The Robert R. Churches of Memphis*, 126.

82. Darlene Clark Hine, "Black Professionals and Race Consciousness: Origins of the Civil Rights Movement, 1890–1950," *Journal of American History* 89, no. 4 (March 2003): 1279.

83. Ibid.

84. Church and Church, *The Robert R. Churches of Memphis*, 120–26.

85. Will Hays to Warren G. Harding, April 21, 1921, Church Family Papers, box 3, folder 33.

86. Kelly, "Robert R. Church," 63.

**Chapter 5. Man of Destiny**

1. L. M. Naughton to Robert Church Jr., June 20, 1923, Church Family Papers, box 4, folder 40. Naughton was the general manager of the Cadillac Motor Car Company and had written Church a letter to thank him for his purchase.

2. Wright, *Race, Power, and Political Emergence in Memphis*, 34; George Washington Lee, "Poetic Memories of Beale Street," *West Tennessee Historical Society Papers* 28 (1969): 65–66.

3. Wright, *Race, Power, and Political Emergence in Memphis*, 34–35; W. C. Handy, *Father of the Blues: An Autobiography* (New York: Macmillan Co., 1942), 86–203.

4. Robert Church Jr. to Sara "Sallie" Church, January 25, 1922, Church Family Papers, box 2, folder 14.

5. *Chicago Defender*, July 8, 1922.

6. Robert Church Jr. to Sara "Sallie" Church, January 25, 1922, Church Family Papers, box 4, folder 14; Church and Church, *The Robert R. Churches of Memphis*, 64.

7. *Baltimore Afro-American*, June 19, 1926; Lewinson, *Race, Class, & Party*, 139; Will Hays to President Warren G. Harding, April 27, 1921, Church Family Papers, box 3, folder 35; applications for Post Office appointments, Church Family Papers, box 5, folder 1, and box 5, folder 20.

8. Melton, "Blacks in Memphis," 96.

9. Sherman, *The Republican Party and Black America*, 135; Kelly, "Robert R. Church," 61–65.

10. Will Hays to Robert Church Jr., Church Family Papers, Correspondence, box 3, folder 35; Church Family Papers, NAACP folder, 1917–68, box 3, folder 31; Biles, *Memphis in the Great Depression*, 97. For more on the activism of the period, see Sullivan, *Lift Every Voice*; Janken, *Walter White*; Johnson, *Along This Way*; Lewis, *When Harlem Was In Vogue*; Colin Grant, *Negro With a Hat: The Rise and Fall of Marcus Garvey* (Oxford, UK: Oxford University Press, 2010).

11. Dowdy, *Mayor Crump Don't Like It*, 13; Lamon, *Black Tennesseans*, 45.

12. Kenneth T. Jackson, *The Ku Klux Klan and the City, 1915–1930* (Oxford, UK: Oxford University Press, 1967), 46; Dowdy, *Mayor Crump Don't Like It*, 38; For more on the Ku Klux Klan, see Nancy Maclean, *Behind the Mask of Chivalry: The Making of the Second Ku Klux Klan* (Oxford, UK: Oxford University Press, 1994), 169.

13. Jackson, *The Ku Klux Klan and the City*, 46–47; Melton, "Blacks in Memphis," 97; Dray, *At the Hands of Persons Unknown*, 233–34.

14. Jackson, *The Ku Klux Klan and the City*, 47; *Commercial Appeal*, April 23, 1923.

15. Melton, "Blacks in Memphis," 97.

16. Letter sent with noosed rope, Church Family Papers, box 4, folder 18.

17. Jackson, *The Ku Klux Klan and the City*, 50–51; Melton, "Blacks in Memphis, 97–98.

18. Ibid.

19. Dowdy, *Mr. Crump Don't Like It*, 39.

20. *Commercial Appeal*, November 2, 1923.

21. Melton, "Blacks in Memphis," 102.

22. Dowdy, *Mayor Crump Don't Like It*, 38–40; Jackson, *The Ku Klux Klan and the City*, 50–54; Lamon, *Black Tennesseans*, 43–44.

23. Dowdy, *Mayor Crump Don't Like It*, 38–40; *Commercial Appeal*, October 28, November 2–3, 1923; Melton, "Blacks in Memphis," 97–99.

24. Lamon, *Black Tennesseans*, 43–44.

25. Gritter, *River of Hope*, 94.

26. Ibid., 45; Melton, "Blacks in Memphis," 100; Roberta Church to Lester Lamon, November 4, 1975, Roberta Church Collection. When Lester Lamon prepared his manuscript for *Black Tennesseans*, he sent advance copies of chapters 2 and 3 to Roberta Church, and she disputed the validity of Church entering into any "understanding, agreement, arrangement, or cooperation" with Crump. This did not deter Lamon, as he documented his claims about the alliance.

27. Sullivan, *Lift Every Voice*, 105.

28. William Pickens to Robert Church, January 12, 1921, Church Family Papers, box 3, folder 31.

29. Robert L. Zangrando, *The NAACP Crusade Against Lynching, 1909–1950* (Philadelphia: Temple University Press, 1980), 62.

30. Ibid., 70–71; Sullivan, *Lift Every Voice*, 109; Johnson, *Along This Way*, 365–71.

31. Johnson, *Along This Way*, 371; Zangrando, *The NAACP Crusade Against Lynching*, 70–71; Sullivan, *Lift Every Voice*, 109.

32. Sullivan, *Lift Every Voice*, 109.

33. Zangrando, *The NAACP Crusade Against Lynching*, 75–76.

34. *Norfolk Journal and Guide*, August 25, 1923.

35. Pete Daniel, "Black Power in the 1920s: The Case of Tuskegee Veterans Hospital," *Journal of Southern History* 36, no. 3 (August 1970): 368–88.

36. Ibid., 373.

37. *Chicago Defender*, September 8, 1923.

38. Kelly, "Robert R. Church," 70. Kelly regularly corresponded with Robert Church Jr., Roberta Church, and George W. Lee as he prepared his thesis.

39. Henry Lincoln Johnson to Robert Church Jr., Church Family Papers, April 13, 1923, box 4, folder 7.

40. Ibid.

41. Sherman, *The Republican Party and Black America*, 158–63; *Savannah Tribune*, September 13, 1923; *Chicago Defender*, September 8, 1923; Daniel, "Black Power in 1920s," 383; Henry Lincoln Johnson to Robert Church Jr., April 13, 1923, Church Family Papers, box 4, folder 7.

42. *Chicago Defender*, September 8, 1923.

43. George Grier Jr. to Robert Abbot, September 7, 1923, Papers of Roscoe Conkling Simmons, box 2, Lincoln League folder.

44. *Chicago Defender*, September 8, 1923.

45. News clipping, no title, no date, Church Family Papers, box 4, folder 19.

46. Carter G. Woodson to Robert Church Jr., November 1, 1921, Church Family Papers, box 4, folder 19.

47. Ibid., March 17, 1922, Church Family Papers, box 4, folder 19.

48. J. B. Bass (editor of the *California Eagle*) to Robert Church Jr., January 19, 1924, Roscoe Conkling Simmons Papers, box 2, Robert Church Jr. Correspondence folder; Roscoe Conkling Simmons to Perry Howard, December 23, 1923, and Henry Lincoln Johnson, December 24, 1923, Roscoe Conkling Simmons Papers, box 2, Robert Church Jr. Correspondence 1920–39 folder.

49. Roscoe Conkling Simmons, Address to the Country, Roscoe Conkling Simmons Papers, box 2, Lincoln League folder; *Norfolk Journal and Guide*, February 23, 1924.

50. *Chicago Defender*, February 16, 1924.

51. Neil R McMillen, "Perry W. Howard, Boss of Black-and-Tan Republicanism in Mississippi, 1924–1960," *Journal of Southern History* 48, no. 2 (May 1982): 205–24.

52. *Chicago Defender*, February 2, 1924.

53. Ibid., February 9, 16, 23, 1924; John T. Adams to Roscoe Conkling Simmons, January 21, 1924, Church Family Papers, box 3, folder 25.

54. *Norfolk Journal and Guide,* February 23, 1924.

55. *Chicago Defender,* February 9, 1924; Gatewood, *Aristocrats of Color,* 182–83.

56. *Chicago Defender,* February 2, 1924.

57. *Baltimore Afro-American,* February 1, 1924.

58. Bernard Eisenberg, "Kelly Miller: The Negro Leader as a Marginal Man," *Journal of Negro History* 45, no. 3 (July 1960): 182–97.

59. *Chicago Defender,* February 16, 1924.

60. Kelly Miller to Robert Church Jr., July 17, 1923, Church Family Papers, box 4, folder 6.

61. Robert Church Jr. to Kelly Miller, July 25, 1923, Church Family Papers, box 4, folder 6.

62. Eisenberg, "Kelly Miller," 187.

63. Ibid.

64. Gilmore, "False Friends and Avowed Enemies," 220–22; Nancy J. Weiss, *Farewell to the Party of Lincoln: Black Politics in the Age of FDR* (Princeton, NJ: Princeton University Press, 1983), 3–12.

65. Gilmore, "False Friends and Avowed Enemies," 219–38. For more on African Americans and the Republican Party, see Weiss, *Farewell to the Party of Lincoln*; Sherman, *The Republican Party and Black America*; and Topping, *Lincoln's Lost Legacy.*

66. Gilmore, "False Friends and Avowed Enemies," 219–38.

67. *Baltimore Afro-American,* January 11, 1924; Lee, *Beale Street,* 262.

68. Lee, *Beale Street,* 262.

69. Ibid.

70. Ibid.

71. Walton, *Black Republicans,* 43; Tucker, *Lieutenant Lee of Beale Street,* 83.

72. *Pittsburgh Courier,* May 3, 1924.

73. Ibid.

74. Lee, *Beale Street,* 264; Tucker, *Lieutenant Lee of Beale Street,* 83.

75. Kelly, "Robert R. Church," 74.

76. *Norfolk Journal and Guide,* June 28, 1924.

77. Church and Church, *The Robert R. Churches of Memphis,* 126; Jackson, *A Chief Lieutenant of the Tuskegee Machine,* 207; Kelly, "Robert R. Church,"75.

78. Sherman, *The Republican Party and Black America,* 205.

79. Kelly, "Robert R. Church," 76; *Chicago Defender,* October 4, 1924.

80. *Chicago Defender,* October 4, 1924.

81. *New York Times,* August 12, 1924.

82. Sherman, *The Republican Party and Black America,* 212.

83. Topping, *Lincoln's Lost Legacy,* 10

84. Sherman, *The Republican Party and Black America,* 213.

85. Topping, *Lincoln's Lost Legacy,* 205.

## Chapter 6. Church Must Go

1. Cherisse Jones-Branch, "Mary Church Terrell (1863–1954): Revisiting the Politics of Race, Class, and Gender," in Sarah Wilkerson Freeman and Beverly Greene Bond, eds., *Tennessee Women: Their Lives and Times* (Athens: University of Georgia Press, 2009), vol. 1: 86–87.

2. Ibid.; Terrell, *A Colored Woman in a White World,* 445.

3. Louisa Ayers Martell (formerly Church) to Robert Church Jr., no date, Church Family Papers, box 2, folder 13; Hamilton, *The Bright Side of Memphis,* 99–101.

4. Mary Church Terrell to Robert Church Jr., January 14, 1926, Church papers, box 3, folder 8; Thomas Church to Robert Church, April 22, 1912, and September 16, 1912, Church Family Papers, box 3, folder 8; Jones-Branch, "Mary Church Terrell," 74.

5. Jones-Branch, "Mary Church Terrell," 75.

6. *Baltimore Afro-American,* June 19, 1926.

7. Lamon, *Black Tennesseans,* 46.

8. Lee, *Beale Street,* 244.

9. *Pittsburgh Courier,* September 17, 1927.

10. Lee, *Beale Street,* 244.

11. Ibid.

12. Gritter, *River of Hope,* 72–73.

13. Lamon, *Black Tennesseans,* 46.

14. Gritter, *River of Hope,* 78.

15. Lee, *Beale Street,* 244–47; Lamon, *Black Tennesseans,* 46; Green, *Battling the Plantation Mentality,* 36; Michael K. Honey, *Southern Labor and Black Civil Rights: Organizing Memphis Workers* (Urbana: University of Illinois Press, 1993), 49; *Pittsburgh Courier,* September 17, 1921.

16. *Pittsburgh Courier,* September 24, 1927.

17. Tucker, *Lieutenant Lee of Beale Street,* 93; Melton, "Blacks in Memphis," 101.

18. Tucker, *Lieutenant Lee of Beale Street,* 93.

19. Dowdy, *Mayor Crump Don't Like It,* 45; Lee, *Beale Street,* 245; Tucker, *Lieutenant Lee of Beale Street,* 94.

20. Dowdy, *Mayor Crump Don't Like It,* 50.

21. *New York Amsterdam,* November 16, 1927.

22. Ibid.

23. Lee, *Beale Street,* 247.

24. Tucker, *Lieutenant Lee of Beale Street,* 95–96.

25. *Commercial Appeal,* September 9 and 10, 1927; Biles, *Memphis in the Great Depression,* 27.

26. Green, *Battling the Plantation Mentality*, 36.

27. Ibid., 36–37; Tucker, *Lieutenant Lee of Beale Street*, 63–64.

28. *New York Amsterdam*, November 16, 1927; Gritter, *River of Hope*, 88.

29. Melton, "Blacks in Memphis," 102.

30. *Chicago Defender*, November 19, 1927.

31. *New York Amsterdam*, November 16, 1927.

32. *Pittsburgh Courier*, November 19, 1927.

33. Ibid., November 26, 1927

34. Robin D. G. Kelley, *Race Rebels: Culture, Politics, and the Black Working Class* (New York: Free Press, 1994), 8–9. Kelley defines "infrapolitics" as the daily confrontations, evasive actions, and stifled thoughts that often inform organized political movements.

35. *Pittsburgh Courier*, November 26, 1927; Manning Marable, *The Great Wells of Democracy: The Meaning of Race in American Life* (New York: BasicCivitas Books, 2002), 68.

36. *Chicago Defender*, July 21, 1928.

37. *Baltimore Afro-American*, March 31, 1928.

38. Ibid.

39. Ibid.

40. *Pittsburgh Courier*, April 7, 1928.

41. Undated news clipping, Church Family Papers, box 5, folder 10.

42. *Commercial Appeal*, March 29, 1928.

43. U.S. Congress, Senate Committee on Post Office and Post Roads, Hearings Before a Subcommittee on Post Offices and Post Roads, 70th Congress., 2nd Session., pp. 47, 120–23.

44. Biles, "Robert R. Church of Memphis," 365; Lewinson, *Race, Class, & Party*, 139; Church and Church, *The Robert R. Churches of Memphis*, 129.

45. Congressional Record, 69th Congress, Session 1, pp. 5346–48, 8459–61 (March 10 and April 29, 1926).

46. McMillen, "Perry W. Howard," 213; *Chicago Defender*, July 21, 1928; *Philadelphia Tribune*, July 26, 1928; *Baltimore Afro-American*, July 28, 1928.

47. *Commercial Appeal*, February 27, 1928.

48. Kelly, "Robert R. Church," 84.

49. Ibid., 86; Biles, "Robert R. Church Jr. of Memphis," 366–67; *New York Times*, June 7, 1928, *Commercial Appeal*, May 30, 1928, *Chicago Defender*, August 11, 1928.

50. *Philadelphia Tribune*, August 2, 1928, *Pittsburgh Courier*, August 11, 1928.

51. Topping, *Lincoln's Lost Legacy*, 12; Tucker, *Lieutenant Lee of Beale Street*, 85.

52. George Mayer, *The Republican Party 1854–1966* (New York: Oxford University Press, 1967), 406.

53. Topping, *Lincoln's Lost Legacy*, 12; Sherman, *The Republican Party and Black America*, 224; Tucker, *Lieutenant Lee of Beale Street*, 85.

54. W. E. B. Du Bois, "POSTSCRIPT," *The Crisis* 35 (November 1928): 381.

55. Sherman, *The Republican Party and Black America*, 224.

56. Ibid.; Herbert Hoover, *Principles of Mining: Valuation, Organization, and Administration; Copper, Gold, Lead, Silver, Tin, and Zinc* (New York: Hill Publishing Co., 1909), 163.

57. Sherman, *The Republican Party and Black America*, 232; Topping, *Lincoln's Lost Legacy*, 12.

58. Robert Church Jr. to Hubert Work, August 15, 1928, Church Family Papers, box 5, folder 7.

59. Unnamed news clippings, no dates, Church Family Papers, box 5, folder 7; *Houston Sentinel*, August 31, 1928, Church Family Papers, box 5, folder 23.

60. Unnamed news clippings, no dates, Church Family Papers, box 5, folder 7.

61. *Pittsburgh Courier*, September 1, 1928.

62. Unnamed news clippings, no dates, Church Family Papers, box 5, folder 7.

63. *Time*, February 18, 1929.

64. Biles, *Memphis in the Great Depression*, 98.

65. G. Michael McCarthy, "Smith vs. Hoover—The Politics of Race in West Tennessee," *Phylon* 39, no. 2 (2nd qtr. 1978): 154–68; *Chicago Defender*, November 3, 1928.

66. *Chicago Defender*, November 3, 1928.

67. Ibid.; Biles, *Memphis in the Great Depression*, 99; Biles, "Robert R. Church Jr. of Memphis," 36; Weiss, *Farewell to the Party of Lincoln*, 12.

68. Sherman, *The Republican Party and Black America*, 233.

69. *Chicago Defender*, March 9, 1928.

70. Unnamed news clipping, no date, Church Family Papers, box 5, folder 23; Topping, *Lincoln's Lost Legacy*, 16.

71. *Commercial Appeal*, March 10, 1929; Sherman, *The Republican Party and Black America*, 234.

72. Hubert Work's assistant to Robert R. Church Jr., May 3, 1929, Church Family Papers, box 3, folder 6.

73. Walter White, *A Man Called White: The Autobiography of Walter White* (Athens: University of Georgia Press, 1995), 102–19; *The Crisis* 37 (July 1930).

74. Robert Church to Herbert Hoover, November 6, 1929, Church Family Papers, box 3, folder 6.

75. Ibid.

76. Kenneth Goings, *"The NAACP Comes of Age": The Defeat of Judge John J. Parker* (Bloomington: Indiana University Press, 1990), 21.

77. Sherman, *The Republican Party and Black America*, 237–38.

78. Goings, *"The NAACP Comes of Age,"* 23–24; Harvard Sitkoff, *A New Deal For Blacks: The Emergence of Civil Rights as a National Issue: The Depression Decade* (Oxford, UK: Oxford University Press, 1978), 85.

79. Gritter, *River of Hope*, 109.

80. *Mid-South Liberator*, June 13, 1931, Church Family Papers, box 6, folder 12.

81. Biles, "Robert R. Church Jr. of Memphis," 362–82.

82. Ibid.; Topping, *Lincoln's Lost Legacy*, 1–28; Gilmore, "False Friends and Avowed Enemies," 219–38.

83. Robert Church to Herbert Hoover, November 6, 1929, Church Family Papers, box 3, folder 6; Weiss, *Farewell to the Party of Lincoln*, 12–33; Gilmore, "False Friends and Avowed Enemies," 219–38.

84. James Weldon Johnson, "A Negro Looks at Politics," in *The Selected Writings of James Weldon Johnson Volume II: Social, Political, and Literary Essays*, ed. Sondra Kathryn Wilson (Oxford, UK: Oxford University Press, 1995), 113.

85. Adkins, "Beale Street Goes to the Polls," 88–89. Adkins interviewed Church on June 11, 1935, and provided the details of their conversation in his thesis.

## Epilogue: The Memphis Blues

1. *Pittsburgh Courier*, May 3, 1952; *Commercial Appeal*, February 27, 1953.

2. *Memphis Press-Scimitar*, March 12, 1953; various news clippings, Church Family Papers, box 10, folder 11; *Chicago Defender*, March 7, 1953; *Memphis World*, November 22, 1940; Church and Church, *The Robert R. Churches of Memphis*, 185; Brewer, "Robert R. Church," 249–51.

3. Adkins, "Beale Street Goes to the Polls," 60, 66–67.

4. Ibid., 87; Biles, "Robert R. Church of Memphis," 377–78.

5. *Kansas City Plain Dealer*, July 14 and 28, 1933; biographical information on Robert Church Jr., Church Family Papers, box 6, folder 45.

6. *Kansas City Plain Dealer*, May 18, 1934.

7. Ibid., May 25, 1934.

8. Biles, "Robert R. Church of Memphis," 362–82; Green, *Battling the Plantation Mentality*, 32–33; Dowdy, *Mayor Crump Don't Like It*, 109.

9. Weiss, *Farewell to the Party of Lincoln*, 97; Janken, *Walter White*, 164–65, 189–91; Sullivan, *Lift Every Voice*, 226–27.

10. Robert Church Jr. to Walter White, November 18, 1931, and January 2, 1932, Papers of Roscoe Conkling Simmons, box 2, Lincoln League folder.

11. Robert Church Jr. to Roscoe Conkling Simmons, January 9, 1932, Roscoe Conkling Simmons Papers, box 2, Robert Church Jr. Correspondence folder; *Chicago Defender*, January 30, 1932.

12. *Chicago Defender*, February 13, 1932.

13. Mary White Ovington to Robert Church Jr., January 15, 1932, Roscoe Conkling Simmons Papers, box 2, Robert Church Jr. Correspondence folder; Robert Church Jr. to Walter White, undated, Roscoe Conkling Simmons Papers, Robert Church Jr. Correspondence folder.

14. Robert Church Jr. to Walter White, February 4, 1932, Roscoe Conkling Simmons Papers, box 2, Robert Church Jr. Correspondence folder; Walter White to

Robert Church Jr., February 17, 1932, Roscoe Conkling Simmons Papers, box 2, Robert Church Jr. Correspondence folder; Robert Church Jr. to Roscoe Conkling Simmons, February 21, 1932, Roscoe Conkling Simmons Papers, box 2, Robert Church Jr. Correspondence folder; *Chicago Defender,* February 13, 1932.

15. Biles, *Memphis in the Great Depression,* 103–4.

16. Tucker, *Lieutenant Lee of Beale Street,* 125; Biles, *Memphis in the Great Depression,* 103.

17. Roberta Church, interview by Charles Crawford, transcript, July 10, 1972, no. 2, pp. 2–3, Mississippi Valley Collection, McWherter Library, University of Memphis.

18. James C. Dickerson to Robert Church Jr., October 30, 1940, Edward Meeman Papers, box 6, E. H. Crump (Misc.) folder, Mississippi Valley Collection, McWherter Library, University of Memphis (qtd. in Biles, "Robert R. Church Jr. of Memphis," 371); Biles, "Robert R. Church Jr. of Memphis," 378.

19. *Commercial Appeal,* February 11, 1940.

20. Wendell Willkie to Robert Church Jr., Church Family Papers, box 6, folder 55; *Memphis Press-Scimitar,* February 10. 1940; *Commercial Appeal,* February 11, 1940.

21. Biles, "Robert R. Church Jr. of Memphis," 379; Tucker, *Lieutenant Lee of Beale Street,* 126.

22. For more on A. Philip Randolph, read Paula F. Pfeffer, *A. Philip Randolph, Pioneer of the Civil Rights Movement* (Baton Rouge: Louisiana State University Press, 1990).

23. A. Philip Randolph to Robert Church Jr., August 6, 1928, Church Family Papers, box 9, folder 4.

24. *Chicago Defender,* November 13 and 27, 1943; Green, *Battling the Plantation Mentality,* 73–75.

25. Pfeffer, *A. Philip Randolph,* 100.

26. A. Philip Randolph to Robert Church Jr., November 18, 1943, Church Family Papers, box 6, folder 53; A. Philip Randolph to Robert Church Jr., December 3, 1946, box 9, folder 4; Alan Knight Chalmers to Robert Church Jr., December 4, 1946, Church Family Papers, box 9, folder 4; Ina Sugihara, "Our Stake in a Permanent FEPC," *The Crisis,* January 1945. Henry Cabot Lodge Jr. to Robert Church Jr., March 19, 1949, Church Family Papers, box 9, folder 4.

27. A. Philip Randolph to Robert Church Jr., April 12, 1949, Church Family Papers, box 9, folder 4.

28. Robert Church Jr. to C. Mason Owlett, April 1, 1949, Church Family Papers, box 9, folder 4.

29. Tucker, *Lieutenant Lee of Beale Street,* 156.

30. Robert Church Jr. to B. Carroll Reece, April 17, 1952, Church Family Papers, box 10, folder 1.

31. *Pittsburgh Courier,* May 3, 1952; *Kansas City Plain Dealer,* April 18, 1952;

*Commercial Appeal,* April 18, 1952. Information on Robert Church Jr.'s death can be found in the Roberta Church Collection, box 6, Robert Church Jr. Obituary Items folder.

32. Various news clippings, Church Family Papers, box 10, folder 9; Robert Church Jr.'s Funeral Program, Church Family Papers, box 10, folder 5; *Chicago Defender,* April 26, 1952.

33. Roy Wilkins, *The California Eagle,* April 24, 1952.

# BIBLIOGRAPHY

**Archival Sources**

Benjamin L. Hooks Public Library, Memphis and Shelby County Room, Memphis.
  Roberta Church Collection.
  Edward Hull Crump Collection.
  George W. Lee Collection.
  Watkins Overton Papers.
Chicago Historical Society.
  Claude Barnett Papers.
Harvard Library, Harvard University Archives.
  Papers of Roscoe Conkling Simmons.
Library of Congress, Manuscripts Division.
  National Association for the Advancement of Colored People Papers.
New York Public Library, Schomburg Center for Research in Black Culture.
  John E. Bruce Papers.
  Ralph J. Bunche Papers.
  William Pickens Papers.
  Asa Philip Randolph Collection.
Tennessee State Archives, Nashville.
  Governor Tom C Rye Papers.
University of Memphis, Ned R. McWherter Library, Mississippi Valley Collection.
  Robert R. Church Family Papers.
  Watkins Overton Papers.

**Periodicals**

*Atlanta Daily World.*
*Baltimore Afro-American.*
*California Eagle.*
*Champion Magazine.*
*Chicago Defender.*
*The Crisis.*

*The Crisis Magazine.*
*Flash Magazine.*
*Indianapolis Recorder.*
*Kansas City Capital Plain Dealer.*
*Memphis Commercial Appeal.*
*Memphis Press-Scimitar.*
*Memphis Triangle.*
*Memphis World.*
*The Messenger.*
*Mid-South Liberator.*
*Nashville Banner.*
*Nashville Globe.*
*National Beacon Light.*
*New Orleans Item.*
*New Orleans Times.*
*Picayune.*
*New York Age.*
*New York Amsterdam News.*
*New York Herald Tribune.*
*New York Times.*
*Norfolk Journal and Guide.*
*Philadelphia Tribune.*
*Savannah Tribune.*
*Time Magazine.*
*Tri-State Defender.*
*Western World Reporter.*
*Wilmington Advocate.*

## Published Works

Adkins, Walter P. "Beale Street Goes to the Polls." MA thesis, Ohio State University, 1935.

Anderson, James D. *The Education of Blacks in the South, 1860–1935.* Chapel Hill: University of North Carolina Press, 1988.

Ayers, Edward. *The Promise of the New South: Life After Reconstruction.* New York: Oxford University Press, 1992.

Baker, Thomas H. *The Memphis Commercial Appeal: A History of a Southern Newspaper.* Baton Rouge: Louisiana State University Press, 1971.

Baker, William. *Jesse Owens: An American Life.* New York: Free Press, 1986.

Biles, Roger. *Memphis in the Great Depression.* Knoxville: University of Tennessee Press, 1986.

———. "Robert R. Church Jr. of Memphis: Black Republican Leader in the Age of

Democratic Ascendancy, 1928–1940." *Tennessee Historical Quarterly* 42 (Winter 1983): 362–82.

Birmingham, Stephen. *Certain People: America's Black Elite*. Boston: Little, Brown, and Co., 1977.

Bond, Beverly Greene. "Roberta Church: Race and the Republican Party in the 1950s." In *Portraits of African American Life Since 1865*, ed. Mjagkij, 181–97.

———. "'Till Fair Aurora Rise'": African-American Women in Memphis, Tennessee, 1840–1915." PhD diss., University of Memphis, 1996.

———, and Janann Sherman. *Memphis in Black and White*. Charleston, SC: Arcadia Publishing, 2003.

Boulware, Marcus. "Roscoe Conkling Simmons: The Golden Voiced Politico." *Negro History Bulletin* 29 (March 1966), 131–32.

Brewer, W. M. "Robert R. Church." *Journal of Negro History* 38 (April 1953): 249–51.

Brown, Elsa Barkley. "Negotiating and Transforming the Public Sphere: African American Political Life in the Transition from Slavery to Freedom. In *Jumpin' Jim Crow*, ed. Dailey, Gilmore, and Simon, 28–66.

Brown, Leslie. *Upbuilding Black Durham: Gender, Class, and Black Community Development in the Jim Crow South*. Chapel Hill: University of North Carolina Press, 2008.

Brundage, W. Fitzhugh. *Lynching in the New South: Georgia and Virginia, 1880–1930*. Urbana: University of Illinois Press, 1993.

———. *The Southern Past: A Clash of Race and Memory*. Cambridge, MA: Harvard University Press, 2005.

Bunche, Ralph J. "The Negro in the Political Life of the United States." *Journal of Negro Education* 10 (July 1941): 567–84.

———. *The Political Status of the Negro in the Age of FDR*. Chicago: University of Chicago Press, 1973.

Capers, Gerald M. *The Biography of a River Town: Memphis, Its Heroic Age*. Chapel Hill: University of North Carolina Press, 1939.

Cartwright, Joseph. *Triumph of Jim Crow: Tennessee Race Relations in the 1880s*. Knoxville: University of Tennessee Press, 1976.

Chafe, William H., Raymond Gavins, and Robert Korstad, eds. *Remembering Jim Crow: African Americans Tell about Life in the Segregated South*. New York: New Press, 2001.

Church, Annette E., and Roberta Church. *The Robert R. Churches of Memphis: A Father and Son Who Achieved in Spite of Race*. Ann Arbor, MI: Edward Brothers, 1974.

Church, Roberta, Charles Crawford, and Ronald Walter, eds. *Nineteenth Century Families of Color, 1850–1900*. Memphis: Murdock Printing Co., 1987.

Cobb, James C. *The Most Southern Place on Earth: The Mississippi Delta and the Roots of Regional Identity*. New York: Oxford University Press, 1992.

Crosby, Molly Caldwell. *The American Plague: The Untold Story of the Yellow Fever, the Epidemic That Shaped Our History.* New York: Berkley Publishing Group, 2006.

Dailey, Jane, Glenda Elizabeth Gilmore, and Bryant Simon, eds. *Jumpin' Jim Crow: Southern Politics from Civil War to Civil Rights.* Princeton, NJ: Princeton University Press, 2000.

Daniel, Pete. "Black Power in the 1920s: The Case of Tuskegee Veterans Hospital." *Journal of Southern History* 36 (August 1970): 368–88.

Decosta-Willis, Miriam, ed. *The Memphis Diary of Ida B. Wells: An Intimate Portrait of the Activist as a Young Woman.* Boston: Beacon Press, 1995.

Dennis, Rutledge M. "Du Bois and the Role of the Educated Elite." *Journal of Negro Education* 46 (Autumn 1977): 388–402.

Dillard, Tom. "Scipio A. Jones." *Arkansas Historical Quarterly* 31 (Autumn 1972): 201–9.

Dowdy, G. Wayne. *Mayor Crump Don't Like It: Machine Politics in Memphis.* Jackson: University Press of Mississippi, 2006.

Du Bois, W. E. B. "Let Us Reason Together." *The Crisis* 18 (September 1919).

———. "POSTSCRIPT." *The Crisis* 35 (November 1928).

———. "Returning Soldiers." *The Crisis* 17 (May 1919).

Duster, Alfreda M., ed. *Crusade for Justice: The Autobiography of Ida B. Wells.* Chicago: University of Chicago Press, 1970.

Dray, Phillip. *At the Hands of Persons Unknown: The Lynching of Black America.* New York: Modern Library, 2002.

Dumenil, Lynn. *Modern Temper: American Culture and Society in the 1920s.* New York: Hill and Wang, 1995.

Egerton, John. *Speak Now Against the Day: The Generation Before the Civil Rights Movement in the South.* Chapel Hill: University of North Carolina Press, 1995.

Eisenberg, Bernard. "Kelly Miller: The Negro Leader as a Marginal Man." *Journal of Negro History* 45 (July 1960): 182–97.

Fairclough, Adam. *Better Day Coming: Blacks and Equality, 1890–2000.* New York: Viking Penguin, 2001.

Foner, Eric. *The Story of American Freedom.* New York: W. W. Norton & Co., 1998.

Franklin, John Hope. *From Slavery to Freedom: A History of African Americans.* 8th ed. New York: Alfred A. Knopf, 2006.

———, and August Meier, eds. *Black Leaders of the Twentieth Century.* Urbana: University of Illinois Press, 1982.

Frazier, E. Franklin. *Black Bourgeoisie: The Rise of a New Middle Class.* New York: Free Press, 1957.

Fredrickson, George M. *The Black Image in the White Mind: The Debate on Afro-American Character and Destiny, 1817–1914.* New York, Harper & Row, 1971.

Freeman, Sarah Wilkerson, and Beverly Greene Bond, eds. *Tennessee Women: Their Lives and Times.* Vol. 1. Athens: University of Georgia Press, 2009.

Gaines, Kevin. "Rethinking Race and Class in African-American Struggles for Equality, 1885–1941." *American Historical Review* 102 (April 1997): 378–87.

———. *Uplifting the Race: Black Leadership, Politics, and Culture in the Twentieth Century.* Chapel Hill: University of North Carolina Press, 1996.

Gatewood, Willard B. "Aristocrats of Color: South and North The Black Elite, 1880–1920." *Journal of Southern History* 54 (February 1988): 3–20.

———. *Aristocrats of Color: The Black Elite, 1880–1920.* Bloomington: Indiana University Press, 1990.

Giddings, Paula J. *IDA: A Sword Among Lions: Ida B. Wells and the Campaign Against Lynching.* New York: HarperCollins Publishers, 2008.

———. *When and Where I Enter: The Impact of Black Women on Race and Sex in America.* New York: HarperCollins, 1996.

Gilmore, Glenda Elizabeth. *Defying Dixie: The Radical Roots of Civil Rights, 1919–1950.* New York: W. W. Norton & Co., 2008.

———. "False Friends and Avowed Enemies: Southern African Americans and Party Allegiances in the 1920s." In *Jumpin' Jim Crow,* ed. Dailey, Gilmore, and Simon, 219–38.

Goings, Kenneth. *"The NAACP Comes of Age": The Defeat of Judge John J. Parker.* Bloomington: Indiana University Press, 1990.

———, and Gerald L. Smith. "Duty of the Hour: African American Communities in Memphis, 1862–1923. In *Trial and Triumph,* ed. Van West, 227–42.

———. "'Unhidden' Transcripts: Memphis and African American Agency, 1862–1920." *Journal of Urban History* 21 (March 1995): 372–94.

Gordon, Ann D., et al., eds. *African American Women and the Vote, 1837–1965.* Amherst: University of Massachusetts Press, 1997.

Goudsouzian, Aram, and Charles W. McKinney Jr. *An Unseen Light: Black Struggles for Freedom in Memphis, Tennessee.* Lexington: University Press of Kentucky, 2018.

Graham, Lawrence Otis. *Our Kind of People: Inside America's Black Upper Class.* New York: HarperCollins Publishers, 1999.

———. *The Senator and the Socialite: The True Story of America's First Black Dynasty.* New York: HarperCollins Publishers, 2006.

Grant, Colin. *Negro with a Hat: The Rise and Fall of Marcus Garvey.* Oxford, UK: Oxford University Press, 2010.

Gritter, Elizabeth. *River of Hope: Black Politics and the Memphis Freedom Movement, 1865–1954.* Lexington: University Press of Kentucky, 2014.

Green, Adam, and Charles Payne, eds. *Time Longer Than Rope: A Century of African American Activism.* New York: New York University Press, 2003.

Green, Laurie. *Battling the Plantation Mentality: Memphis and the Black Freedom Struggle.* Chapel Hill: University of North Carolina Press, 2007.

Hahn, Steven. *A Nation Under Our Feet: Black Political Struggles in the Rural South from Slavery to Migration.* Cambridge, MA: Harvard University Press, 2005.

Hale, Grace Elizabeth. *Making Whiteness: The Culture of Segregation in the South, 1890–1940.* New York: Vintage Books, 1999.

Hamilton, Green Polonius. *The Bright Side of Memphis: A Compendium of Information Concerning the Colored People of Memphis, Tennessee.* Memphis: n.p., 1908.

Handy, W. C. *Father of the Blues: An Autobiography.* New York: Macmillan Co., 1942.

Hardwick, Kevin R. "'Your Old Father Abe Lincoln Is Dead and Damned': Black Soldiers and the Memphis Race Riots of 1866." *Journal of Social History* 27 (Autumn 1999): 109–28.

Harlan, Louis H. *Booker T. Washington: The Wizard of Tuskegee, 1901–1915.* New York: Oxford University Press, 1986.

———, et al., eds. *The Papers of Booker T. Washington.* Urbana: University of Illinois Press, 1976.

Harris-Lacewell, Melissa. *Barbershops, Bibles, and BET: Everyday Talk and Black Political Thought.* Princeton, NJ: Princeton University Press, 2004.

Higginbotham, Evelyn Brooks. *Righteous Discontent: The Women's Movement in the Black Baptist Church, 1880–1920.* Cambridge, MA: Harvard University Press, 1993.

Hine, Darlene Clark. *The African American Odyssey.* 4th ed. Upper Saddle River, NJ: Pearson, 2008.

———. "Black Professionals and Race Consciousness: Origins of the Civil Rights Movement, 1890–1950." *Journal of American History* 89, no. 4 (March 2003): 1279–94.

———. "Rape and the Inner Lives of Black Women in the Middle West: Preliminary Thoughts on a Culture of Dissemblance." *Signs* 14 (Summer 1989): 912–20.

Honey, Michael K. *Southern Labor and Black Civil Rights: Organizing Memphis Workers.* Urbana: University of Illinois Press, 1993.

Hoover, Herbert. *Principles of Mining: Valuation, Organization, and Administration; Copper, Gold, Lead, Silver, Tin, and Zinc.* New York: Hill Publishing Co., 1909.

Ingham, John N., and Lynne B. Feldman. *African-American Business Leaders: A Biographical Dictionary.* Westport, CT: Greenwood Press, 1994.

Jackson, David H. *A Chief Lieutenant of the Tuskegee Machine: Charles Banks of Mississippi.* Gainesville: University Press of Florida, 2002.

Jackson, Kenneth T. *The Ku Klux Klan and the City, 1915–1930.* Oxford, UK: Oxford University Press, 1967.

James, Joy. *Transcending the Talented Tenth: Black Leaders and American Intellectuals.* New York: Routledge, 1997.

Janken, Kenneth Robert. *Rayford W. Logan and the Dilemma of the African-American Intellectual.* Amherst: University of Massachusetts Press, 1993.

———. *Walter White: Mr. NAACP.* Chapel Hill: University of North Carolina Press, 2003.

Johnson, James Weldon. *Along This Way: The Autobiography of James Weldon Johnson.* New York: Penguin Books, 1933.

———. "A Negro Looks at Politics." In *The Selected Writings of James Weldon Johnson Volume II*, ed. Wilson, 113–20.

Jones-Branch, Cherisse. "Mary Church Terrell (1863–1954): Revisiting the Politics of Race, Class, and Gender." In *Tennessee Women*, ed. Freeman and Bond, vol. 1: 68–92.

Kaye, Andrew M. "Colonel Roscoe Conkling Simmons and the Significance of African American Oratory." *Historical Journal* 45 (2002): 79–102.

———. "Roscoe Conkling Simmons and the Mechanics of Black Leadership, 1899–1951." PhD diss., University of Newcastle upon Tyne, 2001.

———. "Roscoe Conkling Simmons and the Mechanics of Black Leadership." *Journal of American Studies* 37 (2003): 79–98.

Kelly, Clarence. "Robert R. Church, a Negro Tennessean, in Republican State and National Politics from 1912–1932." MA thesis, Tennessee Agricultural and Industrial State University, 1954.

Kelley, Robin D. G. *Race Rebels: Culture, Politics, and the Black Working Class*. New York: Free Press, 1994.

Kenneally, James J. "Black Republicans during the New Deal: The Role of Joseph W. Martin, Jr." *Review of Politics* 55 (Winter 1993): 117–39.

Key, V. O., Jr. *Southern Politics: In State and Nation*. New York: Alfred A Knopf, Inc. 1950.

King, Martin Luther, Jr. "Letter from Birmingham Jail." April 16, 1963. www.africa.upenn.edu/Articles_Gen/Letter_Birmingham.html. Accessed April 27, 2005.

Lamon, Lester C. *Black Tennesseans, 1900–1930*. Knoxville: University of Tennessee Press, 1977.

Lawson, Steven F. *Black Ballots: Voting Rights in the South, 1944–1969*. New York: Columbia University Press, 1976.

Lee, George W. *Beale Street: Where the Blues Began*. College Park, MD: McGrath Publishing Co., 1969.

———. "Poetic Memories of Beale Street." *West Tennessee Historical Society Papers* 28 (1969): 64–73.

Lentz-Smith, Adriane. *Freedom Struggles: African Americans and World War I*. Cambridge, MA: Harvard University Press, 2009.

Lewinson, Paul. *Race, Class, & Party: A History of Negro Suffrage and White Politics in the South*. New York: Grosset & Dunlap, 1959.

Lewis, David Levering. *W .E. B. Du Bois: Biography of a Race, 1868–1919*. New York: Henry Holt and Co., 1993.

———. *W. E. B. Du Bois: The Fight for Equality and the American Century, 1919–1963*. New York: Henry Holt and Co., 2000.

———. *When Harlem Was in Vogue*. New York: Penguin Books, 1997.

Lewis, Selma S., and Marjean G. Kremer. *The Angel of Beale Street: A Biography of Julian Ann Hooks*. Memphis: St Luke's Press, 1986.

Lisio, Donald J. *Hoover, Blacks, & Lily-Whites: A Study of Southern Strategies.* Chapel Hill: University of North Carolina Press, 1985.

Litwack, Leon F. *Trouble in Mind: Black Southerners in the Age of Jim Crow.* New York: Vintage Books, 1998.

Logan, Rayford W. *The Betrayal of the Negro from Rutherford B. Hayes to Woodrow Wilson.* New York: Collier Books, 1965.

————. *The Negro in American Life and Thought: The Nadir, 1877–1901.* New York: Dial Press, Inc., 1954.

Lovett, Bobby L. "Memphis Riots: White Reaction in Memphis: May 1865–July 1866." *Tennessee Historical Quarterly* 38 (Spring 1979): 9–33.

Maclean, Nancy. *Behind the Mask of Chivalry: The Making of the Second Ku Klux Klan.* Oxford, UK: Oxford University Press, 1994.

————. *Freedom Is Not Enough: The Opening of the American Workplace.* Cambridge, MA: Harvard University Press, 2006.

Marable, Manning. *The Great Wells of Democracy: The Meaning of Race in American Life.* New York: BasicCivitas Books, 2002.

————. *Race, Reform, and Rebellion: The Second Reconstruction in Black America, 1945–1982.* Jackson: University Press of Mississippi, 1984.

Mays, Benjamin. *Born to Rebel: An Autobiography.* Athens: University of Georgia Press, 1987.

McCarthy, G. Michael. "Smith vs. Hoover—The Politics of Race in West Tennessee." *Phylon* 39, no. 2 (2nd qtr. 1978): 154–68.

McMillen, Neil R. "Perry W. Howard, Boss of Black-and-Tan Republicanism in Mississippi, 1924–1960." *Journal of Southern History* 48 (May 1982): 205–24.

McRae, Donald. *Heroes Without a Country: America's Betrayal of Joe Louis and Jesse Owens.* New York: Ecco Press, 2002.

Melton, Gloria Brown. "Blacks in Memphis, Tennessee, 1920–1955: A Historical Study." PhD diss., Washington State University, 1982.

Miller, William D. *Mr. Crump of Memphis.* Baton Rouge: Louisiana State University Press, 1957.

Mjagkij, Nina, ed. *Portraits of African American Life Since 1865.* Wilmington, DE: Scholarly Resources Inc., 2003.

Moore, Jacqueline M. *Leading the Race: the Transformation of the Black Elite in the Nation's Capital, 1880–1920.* Charlottesville: University Press of Virginia, 1999.

Moses, William Jeremiah. *The Golden Age of Black Nationalism, 1850–1925.* Oxford, UK: Oxford University Press, 1978.

O'Dell, Samuel. "Blacks, the Democratic Party, and the Presidential Election of 1928: A Mild Rejoinder." *Phylon* 48 (1987): 1–11.

Palmer, Pamela ed., "The Robert R. Church Family of Memphis: Guide to the Papers with Selected Facsimiles of Documents and Photographs." Mississippi Valley Collection, McWherter Library, University of Memphis.

Patterson, Orlando. *Rituals of Blood: Consequences of Slavery in Two American Centuries.* Washington, DC: Civitas Counterpoint, 1998.

Pfeffer, Paula F. A. *Philip Randolph, Pioneer of the Civil Rights Movement.* Baton Rouge: Louisiana State University Press, 1990.

Rabinowitz, Harold. *Race Relation in the Urban South, 1865–1890.* Urbana: University of Illinois Press, 1992.

Ritterhouse, Jennifer. *Growing Up Jim Crow: How Black and White Southern Children Learned Race.* Chapel Hill: University of North Carolina Press, 2006.

Rodgers, O. A., Jr. "The Elaine Race Riots of 1919." *Arkansas Historical Quarterly* 19 (Summer 1960): 142–50.

Rushing, Wanda. *Memphis and the Paradox of Place: Globalization in the American South.* Chapel Hill: University of North Carolina Press, 2009.

Ryan, James G. "The Memphis Riot of 1866: Terror in a Black Community During Reconstruction," *Journal of Negro History* 62 (July 1977), 243–57.

Shaw, Stephanie. *What a Woman Ought to Be and to Do: Black Professional Women Workers During the Jim Crow Era.* Chicago: University of Chicago Press, 1995.

Sherman, Richard B. *The Republican Party and Black America from McKinley to Hoover, 1896–1933.* Charlottesville: University Press of Virginia, 1973.

Simmons, Roscoe C. *The Republican Party and American Colored People, 1856–1936.* Chicago: Republican National Committee, 1936.

Sitkoff, Harvard. *A New Deal For Blacks: The Emergence of Civil Rights as a National Issue: The Depression Decade.* Oxford, UK: Oxford University Press, 1978.

Stockley, Grif. *Blood in Their Eyes: The Elaine Race Massacres of 1919.* Fayetteville: University of Arkansas Press, 2001.

Sullivan, Patricia. *Lift Every Voice: The NAACP and the Making of the Civil Rights Movement.* New York: New Press, 2009.

Summers, Martin. *Manliness and Its Discontents: The Black Middle Class and the Transformation of Masculinity, 1900–1930.* Chapel Hill: University of North Carolina Press, 2004.

Sweeney, James R. "The 'Trials' of Shelby County, Tennessee: 'Judge Lynch' Presiding." *Tennessee Historical Quarterly* 63 (2004).

Taylor, Alrutheus A. *The Negro in Tennessee, 1865–1880.* Washington, DC: Associated Publishers, Inc., 1941.

Terborg-Penn, Rosalyn. *African American Women in the Struggle for the Vote, 1850–1920.* Bloomington: Indiana University Press, 1998.

Terrell, Mary Church. *A Colored Woman in a White World.* Amherst, NY: Humanity Books, 2005.

Tolnay, Stewart, and E. M. Beck. *A Festival of Violence: An Analysis of Southern Lynchings, 1882–1930.* Urbana: University of Illinois Press, 1995.

Topping, Simon. *Lincoln's Lost Legacy: The Republican Party and the African American Vote, 1928–1952.* Gainesville: University Press of Florida, 2008.

Tuck, Stephen. *We Ain't What We Ought to Be: The Black Freedom Struggle from Emancipation to Obama*. Cambridge, MA: Harvard University Press, 2010.

Tucker, David. "Black Pride and Negro Business in the 1920's: George Washington Lee of Memphis." *Business History Review* 43 (Winter 1969): 435–51.

———. *Lieutenant Lee of Beale Street*. Nashville: Vanderbilt University Press, 1971.

Van West, Carroll, ed. *Trial and Triumph: Essays in Tennessee's African American History*. Knoxville: University of Tennessee Press, 2002.

Vandiver, Margaret. *Lethal Punishment: Lynchings and Lethal Executions in the South*. New Brunswick, NJ: Rutgers University Press, 2005.

Walton, Hanes, Jr. *Black Republicans: The Politics of the Black and Tans*. Metuchen, NJ: Scarecrow Press, Inc., 1975.

———, and C. Vernon Gray. "Black Politics at the National Republican and Democratic Conventions, 1868–1972." *Phylon* 36 (1975): 269–78.

Weiss, Nancy. *Farewell to the Party of Lincoln: Black Politics in the Age of FDR*. Princeton, NJ: Princeton University Press, 1983.

White, Deborah Gray. *Ar'n't I a Woman? Female Slaves in the Plantation South*. New York: W. W. Norton and Co., 1985.

———. *Too Heavy a Load: Black Women in Defense of Themselves, 1894–1994*. New York: W. W. Norton & Co., 1999.

White, Walter. *A Man Called White: The Autobiography of Walter White*. Athens: University of Georgia Press, 1995.

Williams, Chad Louis. *Torchbearers of Democracy: African American Soldiers in the World War I Era*. Chapel Hill: University of North Carolina Press, 2010.

Wilkins, Roy. *Standing Fast: The Autobiography of Roy Wilkins*. New York: Da Capo Press, 1994.

Wilson, Sondra Kathryn, ed. *Selected Writings of James Weldon Johnson Volume II: Social, Political, and Literary Essay*. Oxford, UK: Oxford University Press, 1995.

Wood, Amy L. *Lynching and Spectacle: Witnessing Racial Violence in America, 1890–1940*. Chapel Hill: University of North Carolina Press, 2009.

Woodruff, Nan E. *American Congo: The African American Freedom Struggle in the Delta*. Cambridge, MA: Harvard University Press, 2003.

———. "The New Negro in the American Congo: World War I and the Elaine, Arkansas Massacre of 1919." In *Time Longer Than Rope*, ed. Green and Payne, 150–78.

Woodward, C. Vann. *Origins of the New South*. Baton Rouge: Louisiana State University Press, 1951.

———. *The Strange Career of Jim Crow*. New York: Oxford University Press, 1955.

Wright, Sharon D. *Race, Power, and Political Emergence in Memphis*. New York: Garland Publishing, Inc., 2000.

Zangrando, Robert L. *The NAACP Crusade Against Lynching, 1909–1950*. Philadelphia: Temple University Press, 1980.

# INDEX

DARIUS J. YOUNG is associate professor of history at Florida A&M University and the founding codirector of the Meek-Eaton Research Center for Social and Political Justice.